For Alison

BLAIRLOGIE BOYHOOD

Robin A. Kelsall

Foreword by Rennie McOwan

Cover: Blairlogie District Tartan, c.1882.
Inset: Author, aged 6, 'helping' Mrs Morris clean her car - one of four in the village at that time. Today, there are over 40.

ISBN 0 9536842 0 2

Published by
Robin Kelsall
Kirklea Cottage
Blairlogie
Stirling FK9 5PX

Typeset by Media Services, University of Stirling

Printed By Russell Print Ltd. 14 Forrest St. Blantyre, Glasgow G72 0JP
Tel: (01698) 821505...Fax: (01698) 710371

Contents

Acknowledgements iv
Dedication v
Foreword vi
Dramatis Personae 1
An Introduction 2
My Parents 4
Blairlogie Village 20
Big Bella 31
Blairlogie Kirk 37
The War 48
Gang Warfare 62
Never Again 68
Farm Days 71
Blairlogie Thistle 79
Uncle Arthur 89
Our Car 93
Gone Forever 101
Bobby's Ball 116
Past Villagers 119
In Conclusion 127

Acknowledgements

For constructive criticism, sound advice and unfailing encouragement, I give my thanks to Kate Durie (Course Tutor at Stirling University), Elma Lindsay (Local History Officer, Stirling Council) and my wife, Benney.

For some of the illustrative material, I'm indebted to Bob McCutcheon, John G. Wilson, Whyler Photos, Marion Peat, Mike Allen, Anna Coull (of New Zealand), the late Nancy Bampton and others. I'm also grateful to Gavin and Terrill Dobson for giving me a sample of the Blairlogie tartan which forms the background to the book's cover.

Finally, thanks are due to my daughter, Fiona. She it was who encouraged me to make use of her PC and introduced me to some of its mysteries. That most of them remain so is not her fault, for I proved a poor and easily muddled pupil. Nevertheless, it made the writing, re-writing and occasional re-re-writing of this wee book hugely less onerous than would, otherwise, have been the case. (I think my late father would have found such an instrument a blessing.)

Really finally, my thanks to my friend Rennie for so readily agreeing to provide a foreword to these reminiscences.

To the Blairlogie girls of the time
who hardly get a mention.

Foreword

Small villages are generally special places. They tend to be scenically attractive, to have long pedigrees and to have a lively social life. Blairlogie is such a place and there is no better person to present an anecdotal and affectionate account of life there than Robin Kelsall.

He was brought up in the village, the son of distinguished parents: writer, historian, broadcaster, actor and conservationist Moultrie and well-known pianist Ruby. He left the area for many years, but the pull of Blairlogie was always strong and he now lives in the village once again.

I have to declare an interest in writing this foreword because, although a Menstrie boy, I was one of several such lads co-opted into the ranks of the Blairlogie Thistle Football squad and paid my thruppence a week until we had enough cash to buy a set of jerseys.

Modern footballers are wimps. Robin still has the signing on chits of yesteryear and we are all still on the books. There was no signing on fee, but there was the occasional post-match feast of lemonade and cakes prepared by sisters and female friends of some of the players. In these days of considering girls to be cissies we ate and drank their fare and then banned them from our premises, a semi-dilapidated cottage, an act which we think of with shame to this day.

The team developed special skills: how to do a wall pass off the real wall which bordered the road without breaking one's foot on the stones, keeping passes and clearances low in case they went dangerously near passing buses or the house windows of the friendly Evans family - two of whose members played in the team - and whose ground (now the car park for Dumyat) we played on. Our fans were asked not to leap up and down too much in the grandstand, an old hen coop, in case it fell apart.

These were memorable boyhood days and Robin brings so much to life. This booklet is a nostalgic read, but even those not born in the Blairlogie area or along the Hillfoots can enjoy it because it is full of knowledge and written with feelings of appreciation for a world that has, to some extent, gone or changed out of recognition.

We were a fortunate generation ... and this booklet gives some of the reasons why.

Rennie McOwan

Dramatis Personae

(in alphabetical order)

Bobby – Robert Muirhead (ex-Manor Croft, Blairlogie.)

Davie – David McLeish (ex-Medrox, Blairlogie.)

Dougie – Douglas Evans (ex-The Orchard, Blairlogie.)

I / Me – Robin Kelsall (Kirklea Cottage, Blairlogie.)

John – John Eadie (ex-Blairmains, Blairlogie.)

Mossie – Maurice Evans (ex-The Orchard, Blairlogie.)

An Introduction

Three, maybe four, years ago, after relating some anecdote anent my boyhood in Blairlogie, one of its more recent residents suggested I should write about it and others of the same period. That sowed the seed and, after a *very* lengthy germination, this is the fruit.

The uncharitable might look on it as a fine conceit to write about my own childhood but, should they read further, I hope they'll discover they misjudge me. With the exception of a couple of clearly personal sections, I am describing a collective boyhood – that of the six or seven of us who, being of broadly similar age, naturally gravitated towards each other. It's just that I've taken it upon myself to act as conduit; I might also add, the main character is really Blairlogie itself.

What's so special about the place? Its size and setting for a start. Think of the smallest village you know and I wouldn't be surprised if it's still bigger than Blairlogie – a church, a shop/post office and a cluster of houses; that was it at the war's end. The only difference today is that the shop/post office is a tea-room. And the setting? The Ochil Hills cut across central Scotland on a west-east axis for twenty-plus miles and they can be seen from a very long way off – notably the southern face which rises sheer from the flat, sea-formed carse. Although steep, these are mainly gentle, green hills with the exception of the knobbly, rocky outpost on the western edge of the range. This is Dumyat and her attendants; one of these, Castle Law, seems to gather the village into her voluminous, rocky skirts.

Huge and solid, she towers over Blairlogie protecting it from all but the very wildest north winds – and even these I suspect. She's a friendly giant although there were two occasions in the past when she forgot herself sufficiently to let slip a clatter of rocks; the second of these nearly killed two of my friends and their family – but that story's for later.

Unless they had a wretched childhood, I imagine many adults of my vintage look fondly on that period in their young lives when, finally trusted to be outwith the range of the all-seeing maternal eye, they were able to explore their environment with their peers and start learning about life – albeit with a very small 'l'. Freedom was something most of us had then. And not just the freedom to go more or less where we chose, but the freedom to get there unthreatened by the excesses of today's traffic and untroubled by the actions of some of today's society.

The hills, the carse and the village itself were our domain – our playground; here, we could indulge in cops-and-robbers or cowboys-and-Indians on a grand scale. (More often than not it was cowboys-and-cowboys – nobody really fancied being one of the Indians.) Both of these were no more than a variation on hide-and-seek with added sound effects. Later, as confidence and ambition grew, there were expeditions to the summits above us – the modest Goats' Craig and Pengower first followed by the more challenging Castle Law and, finally, Dumyat herself – each furnishing our young eyes and imaginations with views to far horizons that not many children had the privilege of experiencing. When the sun was hot enough to warrant the time and effort, we would undertake the fairly considerable hike to Paradise Pool – a spot on Sheriffmuir's Wharry Burn that truly lives up to its name – where we leapt and crashed and splashed in a delirium of delight. (Today, there are signs prohibiting this!)

Of such as these, and others described in this little book, did our Blairlogie boyhood consist. Of *course* there were occasional childish squabbles or disappointments when lips pouted and tears were dashed aside, but my abiding memories are those of an overriding happiness in this idyllic wee place.

But first, let me tell you something of those who introduced me to Blairlogie a lot of years ago...

My Parents

The fact that they were highly talented people meant nothing to me as a child, embarrassed me as a youth – that awkward age when being part of the faceless crowd is all important and they were anything but that – and probably only came to my appreciative notice in my young adult state.

Mother was a pianist of outstanding ability, comfortable in any style though perhaps happiest in what, in the 1920s and 30s, was called Syncopation. In this, and by common consent, she was rated one of the top five female players in Britain. Father was an actor, writer, producer, defender of things Scottish – especially its culture and character – and a bonny fechter against any perceived injustice.

Moultrie Rowe Kelsall was born in Bearsden on October 24, 1904. His father, an engineer well known in Glasgow's industrial circles, was a partner in the firm of Kelsall, Parsons & Co. and inventor of a device known as a 'flywheel equalising booster', the purpose of which was to relieve the load on tramcar-motors during particularly stressful moments. (No, I've not the faintest idea how it did this.) As subsequent events would prove, little of that gentle man's knowledge and ability rubbed off on his son, but the young Moultrie did inherit his mother's way with, and feeling for, words. She was a columnist for the Glasgow Herald, The Scotsman and others, a published writer of plays aimed at the ubiquitous Am. Dram. Socy market and a leading light in the Scottish votes-for-women movement; a woman of strong personality and opinions which she cheerfully shared with many.

Educated at Kelvinside Academy in Glasgow, father readily admitted to never having won a single scholastic prize though he was quite pleased with his athletic successes. The record for the 440 yards which he set in his final year was, I think, still in existence when *I* started at K.A.; certainly, it endured for a surprisingly long time. While he was there, a lifelong love of drama was instilled and nurtured by, of all people, his science-master. Probably an actor manqué, this man not only entertained his pupils with dramatic readings – which might go some way to explaining father's indifference to things scientific – but instigated and developed a school tradition of end-of-term plays. Thus did Moultrie first experience the lure of the lights.

He embarked upon an engineering course, in deference to his father I suppose, at Glasgow University in 1921, but abandoned it after one year declaring that he couldn't get through any class requiring the most elementary knowledge of mathematics. Had he been entirely honest, but this might have been ill-received at home, he would have admitted that he couldn't get through any class which took a back-seat to his acting activities. Within his first year at university he had been offered, and accepted, the part of Theseus in Parry Gunn's production of 'A Midsummer Night's Dream' as a result of which he was invited to join the Scottish National Players – then Scotland's foremost amateur company – with whom he worked for the next seven years. Engineering was oot the windae!

'Following the line of least resistance' (his phrase), he changed to an Eng. Lit. course and was awarded the degree MA. Thereafter, and for no apparent reason other than it seemed a good idea at the time, he took the degree LL B despite having not the slightest interest in law.

In those days, middle-class families tended not to look favourably on the stage as a career for their offspring, especially if there was no back up in the form of a professional qualification in the event of things going sour. My grandparents were no exception so, for a few reluctant years, father went through the motions of pursuing a career in law with the Glasgow firm of McClure, Naismith, Brodie & Co. – still with the SNP on the side of course.

Big decision time was reached in 1928 when Tyrone Guthrie invited him to become professional stage-manager of the Scottish National Players. Actually, it was no big decision at all; he abandoned any pretence of practising the law with delighted alacrity and gave himself wholeheartedly to his new post.

In 1931, Guthrie, who by this time had left for the bigger stages of London, invited father to join the New Westminster Theatre Company in the capacity of actor/publicity manager. This he accepted but, sad at the prospect of leaving Scotland and sadder still when it came to pass, he jumped at an invitation from the BBC to take charge of its Aberdeen station. The offer came when he had been in London for all of two weeks so, allowing for the giving of notice, within five weeks of turning his back on Scotland, he was doing the same on London and heading north to a new job and, unwittingly, my mother-to-be.

On February 1, 1912, Robina Alexander Duncan was born in Aberdeen. The youngest of three children by some distance, her father, a master tailor, had a fairly successful business in the city's Union Terrace. The family she joined had not the slightest musical ability or background, but the infant Ruby (her pet and, later, her professional name) was about to change all that because what it did have was an upright piano.

An essential item in the 'good room' of many households throughout the land, a piano was still the centre of home entertainment in those days; even if the family couldn't play – the case in the Duncan home – it was there for the use of visiting kith or kin who could. Thus was my mother's musical imagination first stirred and stimulated. She used to sit under the keyboard to be as close to the sound as possible and from this position she watched and listened avidly. Proof that it was an unmusical household lay in the fact that between one visitor's performance and the next, the piano was locked – an insurmountable problem to many, but not to a determined three-year-old Ruby.

From her position underneath the keyboard she had worked out the link between different sounds and the rising and falling strips of wood over her head. These were the undersides of the keys – uniform in size and appearance; in other words, no convenient black and white notes to form a diatonic pattern. It must have shocked my grandmother when first she heard sounds coming from the locked instrument; speedy investigation revealed the figure of her tiny daughter kneeling under the keyboard jabbing at the notes above with stubby, enthusiastic fingers. This was impressive but probably no more than the result of intelligent, investigative curiosity; the piano remained locked. The parental minds were soon changed, and quickly, when they recognised a snatch of a tune that had been played by a visitor the previous night; this was something special. From that moment, the lid was up and Ruby had won her place *at,* rather than *under*, the keyboard. There was no stopping her.

She first broadcast at the age of twelve when, having secured the highest marks of any child in Britain in an Associated Board musical examination, she was invited to take part in a Children's Hour from the Aberdeen studios. At fifteen, she won all that could be won in the under-18 category of the 1927 Aberdeen Music Festival and a regular broadcasting spot followed.

This highly satisfactory musical progress was rudely interrupted, indeed threatened, by the sudden death of her father in 1928. The two older brothers had long since left home and though they did what they could financially, there was very little money about – certainly none to spare on luxuries like piano lessons; so my mother did what many had done before and have done since – she got a job. 'Talkies' would shortly revolutionise the film industry, but, at that time, the still silent films needed accompaniment and cinemas needed accompanists; her improvisational skills were ideally suited to this, so she became a silent-movie pianist and, in the process, earned enough to cover her lessons and help out a bit at home.

Within the next couple of years or so, Ruby was to gain her LRAM piano diploma, lose her job at the cinema (the 'talkies' saw to that) and accept the post of house-pianist at the BBC's Belmont Street studios. And then Moultrie arrived.

Aware that the people of Aberdeen and the north-east in general had a collective character and identity unlike that of any other region, he came with the determination to demonstrate this by putting it on the broadcasting map. Opinion had it that, prior to his appointment, the station was best known for its up-to-the-minute herring prices. While these were important to those who lived by them – and, therefore, not to be neglected – he wanted to do so much more. First, though, he had to do something about the staff.

He appears to have inherited two (possibly three) engineers-cum-technicians, a secretary, a cleaning-lady and that was more or less all. Programme-planning dept? *He* was it. Announcers' dept? *He* was it. Sound-effects dept? *He* was it. Public relations dept? *He* was it – and so on. It wasn't long before he was urging that, in order to provide the best for the area, a larger programme staff was required and, if not immediately, he got it.

Father developed an uncanny understanding of the north-eastern mentality – what it wanted in the way of entertainment and what to give it; that perfect blend – neither high- nor low-brow. From the response of the region's listeners, he seems to have got it just right; series such as 'Silver Citizens' – concert-party-type humour and music; 'Facets of Syncopation' – a vehicle for mother's talents and, apparently, much in demand for London Regional, National and Empire programming; 'Radioptimists' – more music, more humour; programmes on the north-east's farming heritage featuring its music and especially its bothy ballads as performed by the peerless John Strachan, Willie Kemp and others; and then Moultrie's own niche, drama and the radio-play in particular. He wrote several of these as part of the

Mother and Father in the Aberdeen days.

"Mainly Magnus" - televised in 1973 at Stirling's MacRobert Theatre to commemorate 50 years of broadcasting in Scotland.
Top: Magnus Magnusson
Middle (left to right): Peggy O'Keefe, Don Whyte, Howard M. Lockhart, Gordon Jackson, Mollie Weir, Canon Sydney McEwan
Front (left to right): Moultrie R. Kelsall, Ruby Duncan, Grace McChlery, Archie P. Lee, Kathleen Garscadden, Willie Joss, Moira Anderson, Rikki Fulton.

station's output including 'This Day', 'Stop Press' and 'Brief Harmony'. Perhaps the most demanding of all – certainly the most time consuming – turned out to be Children's Hour.

In those days, every region in Britain had its band of Uncles and Aunts – the presenters and links-people who guaranteed the smooth operation of programmes aimed at the young. Father wanted something different so, taking a leaf out of the 'Uncle Remus' book, every evening between five and six o' clock, he became Brer Rabbit and along with Miss Mouse (the very talented Addie Ross) and Squirrel (a talking, piano playing creature – Ruby Duncan) they formed the Aberdeen Animals which turned out to be one of the most popular teams ever to contribute to Children's Hour – and not just in the north-east. The trio was helped out by others on many occasions – a dear old lady called Granny Mutch (journalist Christine Crowe; under thirty and rather nice) – her 'brother' Grandfather More (schoolteacher Arthur Black of whom more later) – Howard the Hare (father's new assistant Howard M. Lockhart) *et al.*.

Children loved these programmes and through the Radio Circle, a club for young listeners, they would write to the Animals or send them drawings of how they imagined them. Indeed, when I was going through material from this period in my parents' lives, I came upon a meticulously written notebook of Aberdeen Animals programmes listened to by a girl called Margaret McCulloch. Each entry followed the same format – subject matter and remarks; here's an example.

> Tuesday, 13th Dec., 1932.
> Subject:- The Diverting History of John Gilpin – A Version of the Poem dramatized by Ida Rowe. [**My paternal grandmother, incidentally.**]
> Remarks:-Very, very good. All about John Gilpin – Brer Rabbit being John Gilpin. Miss Mouse & B.R. sang 'Camptown Races' and Brer Rabbit added a "snappy ending". Margaret's name was read out and my letter was mentioned – Squirrel promised to play 'Marigold' next Tuesday.

And the following week...

> Tuesday, 20th Dec., 1932.
> Subject:- Famous Scottish Children – Pet Marjorie by Marion Angus.
> Remarks:-Very interesting. A play was acted with Squirrel as Pet Marjorie and Brer Rabbit as Sir Walter Scott. Miss Mouse sang some of Pet Marjorie's songs. After the play, Squirrel played 'Marigold' for me and it was simply topping. I liked it best of all.

I don't know how old Margaret McCulloch was but she kept a remarkably accurate little journal in terms of spelling, punctuation and general presentation – no apostrophic uncertainties for her! I wonder if she was a typical or an exceptional product of the educational system of the time? Proof of the importance of fish to the area comes in Margaret's account of the programme for Tuesday, 20th June, 1933. Her 'Remarks' section closes with the terse comment...

> As the Herring Fishing Bulletin was coming on there was no time for songs, etc..

From their first meeting, a mutual appreciation seems to have existed but, as it developed into romance, it has to be admitted that Moultrie was less than diligent when it came to nurturing the tender young relationship. In a not uncommon male way, he felt it could look after itself; besides, he had so many other things requiring his attention.

Without being disloyal to my future father and reading between a lot of lines, I gain the impression that, if not conceited, he was, at least, fine pleased with himself – and why not! At the age of twenty-seven, he had total responsibility for running one of the BBC's outposts; his opinion was sought goodness knows how many times a day on how many matters; his wishes were someone else's commands; a good-looking man, his photograph and latest *bon mot* appeared in various newspapers on a pretty regular basis; he was fêted and invited to support all kinds of good works, one of which – conservation – was to become a lifelong love and hobby. In short, he loved the job, the challenges and, of course, being in the public eye (ear, I suppose, in this case).

Just as Moultrie had confidence to spare, so Ruby had more

than her fair share of diffidence. Clearly, when it came to playing her beloved piano, there was no problem, but when it came to her new beloved, there was; she found his outspoken non-conformity rather overpowering and hard to cope with and it went further. A bonny woman, she nevertheless was developing such low self-esteem that she regarded any of her sex who cast a flirtatious eye in Moultrie's direction (and there were quite a few) as a potential threat. Indeed, yearly she went through agonies when, as part of his annual leave, he would join the SNP on its summer tour round Scotland. She knew one or two females in the cast had a crush on him and half expected his return to herald the end of their relationship. She needn't have worried; he was as oblivious of them as he sometimes seemed to be of her.

I'm making her out to be a bit limp when, in reality, she was nothing of the kind – it was just that she was young (nineteen), inexperienced, in love and, to an extent, in awe of him.

Matters got worse when, in 1932, her mother died. I don't think that unhappy lady had ever got over her husband's death and the atmosphere at home would, in all probability, have been one of sadness which was bound to have an effect upon her naturally reserved daughter. So now Ruby was an orphan.

In those days, nice young ladies didn't live on their own – at least that's what the older generation believed – and she was given a roof over her head by the parents of her friend and fellow piano student, Elsa France and, in this happier ambience, things began to look up. Moultrie too, sentimental and responsively sensitive under the otherwise confident surface, showed the other side of his nature – one of solicitude and consideration.

By the following year, it was evident that the relationship was heading for betrothal. Still my poor mother's uncertainties anent her worthiness or her ability to hold her future fiancé's affections against all-comers would bubble to the surface rather too frequently. Reassurance and firm advice concerning these doubts came from Moultrie's brother Keith. Five years younger but, in quite a few ways, rather more perceptive (sensible even), he wrote to her at the end of April, 1933 and pulled few punches...

> 'Cut out all the "unattractive-ordinary-girl-like-me" stuff. ... Furthermore, you have two qualities which all the others [**former girlfriends**] lacked – an attractive personality and a disarming honesty which is bound to appeal to Moultrie. ... If he shows signs of hankering after other girls, 'phone me and the matter will be put right. ... And I'm sure he'll never be happy without someone to compose music to his lyrics. ...'

...and much more. Thus spake the future Emeritus Professor of Sociological Studies at Sheffield University.

On 13th June, 1933, Moultrie Kelsall and Ruby Duncan – Brer Rabbit and Squirrel – plighted their troth; an event reported in newspapers throughout the land and Margaret McCulloch's notebook.

On 2nd June, 1934, Moultrie Kelsall and Ruby Duncan – still Brer Rabbit and Squirrel – were married in St James' Episcopal Church, Aberdeen. Again, the papers were full of it (after all, this was the stuff of showbiz albeit on a regional scale) but Margaret McCulloch was, by this time, on a new notebook which I haven't seen.

Even on this happy day, misfortune stalked my mother – her late father's brother, also a master tailor, died during the service. Apparently he had travelled north despite feeling poorly and, while sitting in church, had taken a turn for the worse. He was able to walk to a room downstairs where he was made comfortable but, as the papers put it...'His condition was so critical that he expired almost immediately.' News of this tragic incident was kept from all but a few which is why the principals appear so cheery at the church door. Inevitably, it leaked out and by the time of the reception at the Palace Hotel, it was known to all. The guests sat down to lunch but, as soon as it was over, they quickly and quietly left.

Despite an inauspicious start to their new life, the marital state seems to have suited them well. They set up home in rented accommodation in Cults – then a separate village, but now part of the Aberdeen conurbation. The house was called Barclay Well; I've no idea what it looked like, how old it was or anything. All I know is that, eventually, I was born there.

Work both in and out of the BBC occupied them fully; I suppose 'out' applied more to mother than father. She did quite a bit of theatre work, and shows in which she accompanied such as the Laird o' Inversnecky himself (comedian, Harry Gordon) at the Pavilion in Aberdeen featured often in diaries of the time. But BBC duties provided most of her income and herein lay a small problem. Because she was by far the best in the region, she garnered most of the work which led to envy and jealousy in some others. This was expressed through one or two poison pen letters in which charges of outright favouritism and blatant nepotism were levelled and general dislike articulated. Unpleasant, but mercifully short-lived.

During September, 1935, youthful listeners to Aberdeen Animals were dismayed to hear, at one point, that Squirrel had scampered off to London town. She didn't stay very long, however, and the result of her visit was the staggered release of a couple of gramophone records she'd cut at the Columbia studios. That she was a product of the provinces was evinced by the following critique from some southern journal of the time.

> **Radio Artist Mystery**
> Who is Ruby Duncan who made such a delightful piano record last month and has followed it with equally delightful medleys called "Three of Hearts" and "Good Girls"?
> She has a limpid, subtle simplicity of style which is very pleasant to the ear and I recommend Columbia FR 1193 with some confidence. All I can find out about her is that "she is the Doris Arnold of Scottish Regional."

And who was Doris Arnold? I suppose the obvious riposte would be "the Ruby Duncan of London Regional."

I made it into this world at 11.55am on Saturday, 4th January, 1936. I know this because all the information is contained in a diary of events surrounding my birth which mother kept most diligently from 1st Jan., 1936 to 5th Feb., 1936. What happened after this I know not which, in many ways, is a shame, but no more than I would expect. As a family, we've never been of the 'Dear Diary' sort; the date and time of the next gig or rehearsal – so-and-so's birthday – holiday dates – that's the important stuff. Nevertheless, for the few days in which she felt moved to record everything, an entry for Wednesday, 15th Jan. appeals to me...

> Nurse thinks Baby is beginning to see and hear. He certainly looks very intelligently at you.

That's a mother for you; nobody's ever said the like since.

Her confinement highlighted an interesting example of 1930's medical thinking. A smoker, she was positively encouraged to continue the habit in order to ensure a neat and manageable foetal development. When I was plonked on the post-birth scales, they registered 10lb. which led to some scratching of learned heads.

The month of May, 1937 heralded a change of direction for the Kelsall family. After almost six years in charge of the Aberdeen station during which he had totally transformed it, father had now been head-hunted by the infant television service down in London. Reluctantly and with great sadness, my parents prepared themselves for this step into the more or less unknown. At the informal ceremony attended by fifty-odd technicians, artists and writers who had gathered to pay them tribute, father expressed his great affection for the place and its people... "I shout about your architecture and your complacency as Aberdonians [a reference to some lengthy newspaper articles he had written on these very topics]; all the same, I do sincerely think that Aberdonians are pretty nearly the salt of the earth and, Glaswegian that I am, I think I have found more kind hearts and solid worth here than anywhere else I have been..."

And so we said goodbye to Aberdeen – well, father said it first; mother and I had to deal with Barclay Well and other bits and pieces. Some few weeks later, we joined him at our new address – 95, Fortis Green, Muswell Hill (again, rented) – just behind Alexandra Palace where father was now in charge of dramatic and musical productions for television.

Sixty years ago, TV was *tiny*; the actual service in operation was effective only in and around London with an apparent limit of 40-50 miles radius from the Alexandra Palace transmitter. Within this small circle there were, to begin with, about four hundred sets, so the televisual output was probably aimed at two or three thousand people assuming that those *with* were kind enough to invite some of those *without*, occasionally, to share in their viewing. By the end of 1937, over two thousand were estimated to be in use and the BBC could pride itself on being the only organisation in the world which was putting out a regular daily programme.

Many early TV sets – the BBC provided us with one, so I'm speaking from childhood experience – would appear very strange to a modern viewer. Because, initially, of the depth of the cathode-ray tube, it was impracticable to design a forward facing set; its very dimensions would have made it uncomfortably intrusive in all but the largest room. This problem was overcome cleverly and neatly. The tube was placed vertically with the screen pointing to the ceiling and round this was built a free-standing cabinet containing all the other bits and pieces. When the lid was lifted, one looked down onto a deck which accommodated the screen and basic controls. Inside the lid was a mirror, so viewers (called 'lookers' in the early days) were able to sit back, as we do today, but they watched a reflected image – cunning. Technological development was rapid, however, and dimensions and cost were soon made more acceptable. As a result, by August, 1939, there was thought to be upwards of twenty thousand sets in that still small circle. And the quality? Early pictures tended to flicker, though this was eliminated within a year or so and, because of a lack of focus-depth in the cameras, backgrounds were inclined to be fuzzy. In order to achieve good black and white definition for those viewing, it was found that the best transmitting colour was a kind of steel grey, so that became the predominant studio colour in sets *and* make-up.

As soon as was practicable, mother found herself a nice little niche in London's west-end theatreland. A popular form of pre-war entertainment was the revue – a song and dance and sketch type of show satirising current events, fads and conceits – usually mercilessly. The Gate Theatre, small and struggling, was converted into a private membership theatre-club and revue became its highly successful forte; indeed, so successful that it wasn't long before it was doing a regular stint in the larger Ambassadors Theatre though still calling itself 'The Gate Revue'. Music was provided by two pianos (Charles Zwar and Ruby Duncan) and drums (Anthony Spurgin) while the cast variously contained talents destined to become pretty big-time although they may not mean much to those at present under fifty; people like Michael Wilding, Hermione Gingold, Robert Helpmann, Rex Harrison, Godfrey Winn, Beverley Nichols *et al.*.

With both parents working what can only be called anti-social hours, small Robin required someone to look after him and wipe his nose and aught else needing attention. So it was that Mary joined our household in the role of Nanny, not that I ever addressed her as such. In spite of developing a fond attachment, I know little about her save that she had a daughter – the result of a very brief liaison – who was being looked after by Mary's parents on their small farm somewhere in Scotland; I was to become familiar with it fairly soon and quite unexpectedly.

About this time, we bought a car (an Invicta – more on her later) for the purpose of family jaunts and holidays in which Kent and Essex were explored in some detail. I think, too, there lurked at the back of father's mind the thought that she'd be useful as a means of escape from London when the still distant threat of war became a reality.

The Munich Crisis of September, 1938 was the first in a series of events which would culminate in the Second World War a year later. Briefly, there had existed within the BBC a feeling that it might have to close down completely during a future war for fear that 'broadcast emissions' might be capable of guiding hostile aircraft along the wireless beams to their targets. Since it was recognised that broadcasting would play a vital part in any future emergency in terms of boosting national morale, disseminating vital information and countering enemy propaganda, a way round the problem was evolved; this, however, did not apply to TV broadcasts.

The London area viewers were growing in number and enjoying what they watched; hopes of spreading out into the provinces were increasing – then came the blow. On the morning of 1st September,1939, the engineer in charge at Alexandra Palace received a message at 10am; the station must be closed down by noon. The last item to be televised for many years was a Mickey Mouse cartoon; there was no closing announcement – father was out of a job.

It may well be that I was already with Mary on her parents' farm by the time of the TV shutdown; certainly, since war seemed ready to erupt at any time, my parents would have wanted their precious bundle away from the prime target that London could shortly become; they, meanwhile, stayed on at Fortis Green – mother was still at the Ambassadors Theatre and father, presumably, was involved in some sort of decommissioning/mothballing exercise at Alexandra Palace. How long we were apart I don't know, but I *do* know that a perfectly innocent question of mine speedily brought us together again.

After listening carefully to Mary reading a letter sent to me by my mother, I apparently asked..."What does Mummy look like?" Clearly, this kind of question can be misunderstood. Is the child asking it unhappy, thick or merely making conversation? When Mary related the incident to my horrified mother, she had no doubts and the outcome was almost instantaneous – goodbye, London.

Father managed to get a post as acting-Head of Drama (Scotland) at Broadcasting House, Glasgow and, since Mary had decided to help her parents on the farm and be with her daughter at the same time, mother reverted to being... well, a mother.

Yet again, we were living in rented accommodation (a cottage at Portencross near West Kilbride) but, by then, my parents were hankering after a place of their own – something elderly – something with character – something in a country setting – something not too terribly far from Glasgow.

In late 1940 they discovered just what they had been looking for – Kirklea Cottage, Blairlogie.

Kirklea Cottage, Blairlogie as my parents would first have seen it

Blairlogie Village

I remember a feeling of boyish pride when first I saw Blairlogie marked on a Bartholomew large scale map of part of mid-Scotland. There, beside the road to St Andrews and at a contour point where the brown of the hills gave way to the green of the carse, was the legend 'Blairlogie' with a cross and a couple of dots beside it denoting a church and a few houses. Why the pride? Loyalty, I suppose. It's a fairly unusual child who doesn't seek anonymity on most occasions, but it's a very unusual child who doesn't develop an almost proprietorial loyalty towards the place in which he or she lives; I was no exception. Blairlogie's appearance on this map, therefore, gave notice to the world at large (or at least to the mid-Scotland part of the world) that it existed and I was glad.

Blairlogie is by far the smallest of the main settlements dotted along the Hillfoots, but it was not always so. Back in the mid-18th century, the village was as big as some of them – so, what happened? Well, it was all to do with water-power. The industrial entrepreneurs of the 19th century saw the potential in the torrents that tumbled down the steep Ochil slopes at Menstrie, Alva, Tillicoultry and Dollar; Blairlogie's burn, being considerably smaller, just didn't have the volume of water worth harnessing, so, while the other hamlets relentlessly sprouted mills and new housing and more and more people, Blairlogie remained pretty much the same size. Large or small, however, each village demonstrates a similar evolutionary pattern and this is perhaps more readily discernible in Blairlogie because of its lack of sprawl.

The old, or back, road looking west...

... and from further east

Prior to the early 19th century when the flat carse land to the south of the Ochils was a largely undrained, unreliable area prone to severe winter-flooding, travellers kept their feet dry by following tracks and paths along the higher ground at the foot of the hills. One of these became the road which was to link Stirling with Dollar and points east; for the most part, it was a good one too. In his treatise on the agriculture of Clackmannanshire written in 1795, John Francis Erskine of Mar says of it...

> The roads in this district were, in general, uncommonly bad except that running along the foot of the Ochils which, though too narrow, is, for the greatest part, pleasant enough; but here and there, it requires some alteration. As the soil is particularly well adapted for roads, a very little attention and expense might make this road and keep it in excellent repair.

At the time of his writing, this part of the King's Highway was a statute-labour road which meant that responsibility for keeping it in some sort of order fell upon the local inhabitants and, invariably, the poorer ones at that. This well intended but less than successful system of maintenance required that parishioners should carry out six days of roadworks per year. If you had a bit of money, you could pay someone else to do your stint; if you owned property over a certain value, you supervised the work; if you had neither of these, you risked a pretty hefty fine if you failed in your obligation. As a result, statute-labour roads tended to be pretty poor things looked after, as they were, by a largely unskilled and unenthusiastic work-force; of course, if the road was naturally well-bedded and well-drained, it had a great advantage. This was the case with the early Hillfoots road.

The Earl of Mar, in his otherwise favourable reference to the old Hillfoots road, had suggested that it was a bit on the narrow side and so, possibly in response to the demands of the industrialists of the time and in order to attract others, a new turnpike (the *present* Hillfoots road) was constructed in 1806. Built on the recently drained carse land, it had the triple advantage of being wide, straight and level – all comparatively.

Thus the old road became redundant, except for the Menstrie to Alva section, and all but disappeared – notably between Logie and Blairlogie; being fairly close to the new road at this point, both surface and bedding of the old were simply lifted and transferred to the new. Each of the main settlements has, therefore, developed in a similar manner – the oldest part is always higher up alongside the old (or 'back') road while the lower, new road is bordered by comparatively newer building. So it is with Blairlogie.

That it has been around for a long time, there's no doubt and, over the years, the name has undergone some changes – Blarlogy to Blairloggy to Blair of Logy to Blair Logie and the present Blairlogie. Sadly, any evidence of human activity before 1543 has long vanished; in that year, Alexander Spittal (whose family, before and after him, had long connections with the village) built a small, castellated mansion on a plateau near the mouth of Blairlogie Glen. His son, Adam, added an east wing in 1582 thus creating the present L-shaped building.

The next visible stage of Blairlogie's development involves a leap forward to, roughly, the mid-18th century and buildings of this period are much in evidence. They line the old road – The King's Highway – and Kirk Green Road which seems to be the name given to the road running through the village; this was an extension of the loan from the carse south of Blairlogie which enabled the farms and farmlets to connect with either the low road (Stirling to Alloa – a quagmire in winter) or the old Hillfoots road (already praised). The southern boundary of the village at this time appears to have been marked by the Kirk and Manse, but then came the new turnpike. With splendid indifference, it sliced through the loan-cum-village road and a couple of gardens unfortunate enough to get in its way and thus became Blairlogie's new boundary.

Draining the carse produced a better quality of land and more of it which, in turn, encouraged the formation of bigger farm units and, ultimately, the disappearance of smaller ones. Thus today's farms at either end of Manor Loan – Blairmains (originally Blairlogie Mains) and Manor (originally Overtown)

Looking up Kirk Green Road to the Square.
The thatched cottage (middle left) now has a second storey. c. 1900.

Looking along Victoria Place (on left) with Burnside Cottage to the right of Kirklea's lean-to.

– which were built within the first half of the 19th century swallowed up the smaller and older farmsteads of Park and Longkerse. These used to be where the copses are halfway down the loan.

With the exception of Blairmains, the cottages in the angle of the southern and eastern lines of turnpike and loan respectively and the rebuilt kirk, the Blairlogie shown on the Ordnance Survey map of 1864 probably looked little different from that of a hundred-plus years before. By the time of the OS map of 1898, however, changes had taken place. Old was swept aside to make way for new in-filling in the shape of the Manse, Telford House (beside the old road at the back of the village) and Blairlogie Park (immediately east of the present car-park), while previously virgin land now sprouted Struan, Ochil Neuk and Nethercraig; the latter became the village's second post office – the first being the westernmost of the aforementioned cottages immediately south of the turnpike.

Twentieth century development occurred in two stages – **i)** between the wars when four bungalows (two on either side of the farm cottages) were built south of the main road and **ii)** post-war which saw a little flurry of activity in the shape of a two-storey house behind the bungalows to the west, another bungalow opposite the car-park and an unhappily, short-lived little steading on the actual site of the car-park. The most recent building perches on higher ground at the back of the village. It started life as a pre-war animal pen, was converted into a post-war office by a megalomaniac of a man (who shall, clearly, remain nameless) and, two developments later, it became the substantial, if slightly unsympathetic, dwelling-house it is now.

Between 1864 (first OS map) and now (1998) Blairlogie appears to have gained about a dozen buildings and lost the same number which is really quite extraordinary. Indeed, if one could wave a magic wand and remove the myriad cars that litter the village road and, perhaps, disguise the most recent addition to the housing stock, someone who had not seen Blairlogie for fifty years would notice mainly cosmetic changes – little structural. Similarly, and were it possible, one who had last seen the village a hundred years ago and was fearless enough to stand on the north side of the main road with his back to the thundering traffic and the twentieth century building on the other side would be aware of little different. Such could never be said of Menstrie, Alva or any other of Blairlogie's big neighbours.

And what of the people who have lived in this well-favoured spot? How did they earn their bread? Two hundred years ago, most would have worked on the land either as gardeners or farm-workers; a few were tradesmen and, surprisingly, quite a few more were leather-workers. The soutars of Blairlogie made footwear in their own homes for a factory-cum-distribution centre in Blackford to the north of the Ochils. John R. Allan, himself a resident of the village on *two* occasions, describes them thus in his book 'Summer in Scotland'...

> On a set day, perhaps once a fortnight or oftener, each made a pack of his finished work and carried it to the factory. There they were paid for what they had done and were given out more leather. Now here is a curious thing. The journey to Blackford could be walked in a single day, but the long road home took two. There must have been some brave nights at the inn that stands at Sheriffmuir, and the ghosts of the Jacobites who fell in battle there must have sighed happily in their graves, knowing that one old custom was still honoured in their land...

and he continues...

> There were many evils in the old system, for the provident merchant could always exploit the improvident craftsman, but a man could at least work in a natural rhythm according to the seasons. ... Farmers cut their corn with the scythe in those days, so they needed many extra hands in harvest. It was the rule then that the craftsmen put by their tools and worked in the fields, even contracting with the farmer for the labour of all their family.

...now, isn't that a sensible way to organise your year?

In the second Statistical Account of 1841, Rev. William

The megalomaniac referred to lived in this house. Having bought the lanes to east and west and the Square, he was incensed when a hole appeared in the latter. This imperious sign was the result.

The road to Blairlogie from Logie crossroads. The A91 was a long way from re-alignment and, clearly, vehicle saturation point.

Robertson, who compiled the section on Logie Parish, had this to say of the locals...

> The people are in general cleanly in their habits, especially in those villages which are frequented by strangers in summer...

Blairlogie was just such a village. Well before Bridge of Allan developed into a spa and health resort, local physicians were recommending their better off patients to sample the air, orchards and goats' whey of Blairlogie. Apparently, there was quite a herd of the creatures browsing contentedly among the herbage on the aptly named Goats' Craig (behind the castle) and its near neighbour, Pengower, to the west. The latter name, incidentally, is a remnant of an ancient Pictish influence in the area – it means Goats' Craig! The village was fortunate in that many of its houses were of two storeys – ideal for accommodating paying guests – so, each spring and summer, pale consumptives and sufferers of the vapours and other indeterminate, early 19th century conditions were to be seen in the neighbourhood eating and supping produce of orchards and goats and filling their lungs with good hill air. A useful source of additional income for the locals but one that suffered when Airthrey's mineral springs started to flow commercially.

In 1912, Manor Powis colliery opened for business thus providing a further outlet for employment. Admittedly, mine owners of the time probably preferred to import their hewers of coal ready formed, so to speak, but there were all kinds of surface jobs available and, at a mile and a bit down Manor Loan, it was a good opportunity for the inhabitants of Blairlogie.

When we came to live in the village, therefore, the great majority of the employed either worked on or under the land – farming and gardening or mining; a few were professional or in business and a very few more retired or of private means. How different things are today. The mine closed down years ago – even the once conspicuous bing has all but disappeared; farming has retreated into its machine-intensive shell – any

1998. Mrs Fraser Mitchell outside her tea-room...

... and Mrs William Richie outside hers in 1910.

Boghead (now called Fenham). Briefly, in the late 40's or early 50's, Mrs McPhee - the figure at the front door - turned her best room into a tea-room. Blairlogie seems to have a thing about tea-rooms.

extra hands called for are provided by agricultural contractors – and, with the honourable exception of the part-owner of the highly successful Puddleducks tea-room, there's not a working gardener in sight. In short, Blairlogie is now given over entirely to the professional and retired classes – the human population is down, but the automotive one is way, way up. More's the pity!

Big Bella

During the war years, when many young men were in one or other of the armed services, Walter Alexander's buses were run by older men and by women – the former sat in noisy, fume-laden isolation in the driver's cab, while the latter collected fares and generally kept a watchful eye on events in the lower and upper saloons as the passenger accommodation was rather grandly called. Big Bella was one of that band of decent, conscientious, no-nonsense conductresses who made bus travel safe and secure for young and old alike. Although it would never be used to her face, the sobriquet was adopted in order to avoid confusion with a similarly named, but shorter, colleague; predictably, she was Wee Bella.

In the wake of a first and conspicuously unsuccessful attempt to kick-start my education, the parents, after careful consultation, decided to send me to Riverview, a school in Alloa. This tiny establishment was run by Mrs Janet Grieve and her husband along the lines of the system devised by Dr Maria Montessori. In this, the child is encouraged to define its own interests and disciplines rather than having them directed and strictly controlled by a teacher; fine in principle, but fairly useless for idle dreamers like me. I'm told that, having proclaimed my mastery of 'sums', I offered to demonstrate this new skill to my parents. Armed with paper, pencil and ruler, I wrote a digit, placed another underneath, drew a line, wrote another digit under that and then, neatly, drew a cross beside it. As ambition and confidence grew, sums

Mrs Janet Grieve (clearly an early feminist) with some of Riverview's pupils. On the right is a my very first girlfriend.

Looking for Blairlogie? I was being relieved of my tonsils at the time, thus missing the entire photo-call.

involving single digits gave way to tens then hundreds then thousands (not that I realised this). With a flamboyance born of the certainty that my parents' looks of amazement as they regarded paper, me and each other indicated their deep admiration, I was soon doing sums incorporating whole rows of numbers – each with its neatly drawn cross. In a strangely small voice, father asked about the crosses. His very question showed that he knew nothing about sums; putting down the pencil, I gave him my full attention and Rule One... "*All* sums has exes!"... displaying a grasp of grammar marginally less confused than my understanding of arithmetic. A day or so later, and to my surprise, my teacher took me to one side and we spent a long time doing sums. Equally surprising, crosses no longer seemed mandatory; a new sign appeared quite often – a tick.

The school was about half-a-mile from Alloa bus-station, so it was arranged that Mr Grieve's elderly father (known to all as Pop) would meet me and, at the end of the late-starting, early-finishing day, deliver me back to the bus for home. This meant that the potential for mishap was confined to the actual journey; aware that her unworldly son was quite capable of getting lost anywhere between Blairlogie and Alloa, my poor mother elected to accompany me, hand me over to Pop and get the same bus home. This twice-a-day chore – a total of thirty six miles and two-and-a-bit hours travelling time – was rather beyond the duty of responsible motherhood; within two or three days, Big Bella had convinced her of this. From then on, the burden was reduced to putting me on the morning bus and meeting me off the afternoon one. So, over a four year period, Big Bella and I became chums and, one incident apart, developed a fond relationship.

The writer and journalist John R. Allan lived in Blairlogie at this time; he and his wife, poet Jean Mackie, pre-dated our arrival in the village by some three or four years; indeed, they were responsible for introducing my parents to the place and, possibly, to the cottage in which Kelsalls have lived ever since. They had one child a year or two younger than me and when he became of school age, they too decided to send him to Riverview.

Charlie was a happy, chatty, curly-headed cherub who first awakened within me the sensation of jealousy although I couldn't have put a name to it. Until he joined me on the daily journey, I was the one who put the smile on Bella's face and the twinkle in her eye; I was the one occasionally allowed to turn the handle on her ticket machine; I was the one who was given some of the unused tickets when she put a new bundle in the holder. Charlie changed some of that; not all of it, because Bella was too wise to leave me out of things, but enough to persuade me that it would have been better were Charlie not there.

At the end of the lower saloon gangway and centrally placed on the bulkhead beyond which was the engine and the driver's cab, there was a projecting, circular heater; this was my steering wheel. Often I would spend much of the journey with hands on the shiny-rimmed heater and eyes on Jock, Bella's driver. Although the steering was gear-assisted, it still looked physically demanding to haul the great vehicle round a corner; as Jock heaved the wheel through several revolutions, so did I imitate him on the heater. It wasn't long before Charlie wanted some of this particular action; resisting his attempt to push in, I kept hands and eyes resolutely on heater and Jock. At the wail and the shrill complaint...

"He winna gie me a shottie" (Charlie was of north-east stock), I correctly anticipated trouble. Bella's firm tones resounded from the far end of the saloon.

"Don't be so selfish Robin; give wee Charlie a go."

Resentment seeping out of every pore, I moved aside and watched with lip-curling disdain as Charlie's little hands flapped at the heater without any of the imitative and synchronised perfection *I* brought to the task. Fortunately, his interest in the game was as short as he was and soon he lurched back down the gangway towards Bella, smiling endearingly at each passenger on the way. Charlie was a charmer, but it didn't work on me. Things came to a distressing pass one hot, summer's afternoon. It could be that he wanted a break from the two girnin' weans, but for whatever reason, Pop was unable to walk us down to the bus-station.

Between school-day-end and bus-journey-start, there was an interval of about quarter of an hour. Pop's method of ensuring we made it in time was to take Charlie by the hand and more or less pull him along with me trotting by his side. Even though responsibility for getting us safely to Bella's Hillfoots bus had been placed on my narrow shoulders, there was no way I was going to hold Charlie's hand. Children didn't have watches in those days, but experience told me that we had to keep moving. Charlie didn't and wouldn't; he got slower and slower until I had visions of the bus leaving without us. I started to shout at him which proved manifestly counter-productive. His lower lip trembled then collapsed; the ensuing wail contained the information... "Ma wee leggies winna go ony faster." I considered this statement grimly and then pointed out, quite reasonably I thought, that if he wished to miss the bus, I didn't and, further, if he was not prepared to get his 'wee leggies' pumping, I was going to leave him. And so this wailing, shouting vision of childish intransigence made a slow, unsteady progress towards Bella and safe-home.

My last pretence at patience evaporated when we were actually quite close to our goal – just a corner away in fact. Charlie sat down, still wailing, and refused to go any further; deciding on action rather than threat, I informed him that that was it and I was off; the wail reached an alarming pitch. As much to escape the racket as anything, I hared round the corner just in time to see our vehicle slowly leaving its stance. Bella's three-bell emergency signal brought this movement to an immediate halt.

"Hurry up, Robin. You're late;" she shouted and then, inevitably, "where's wee Charlie?"

By this time, *my* lower lip was trembling and it, too, collapsed. Between sobs, I blurted out that he wouldn't hurry and that I'd left him round the corner.

"Get in there and sit down." Bella's voice was rising ominously; wretchedly and hurriedly I obeyed.

Through my tears I watched the small figure of Charlie appear round the corner, shirt-tail out, socks down to shoe level, wee baggie dragging behind him.

"Come away ma wee lamb," cooed Bella. "What's Robin been doin' t'you?"

The bus started and within minutes Charlie was chuckling away, smiling up at Bella with big eyes. My misery was now complete; would she tell on me when we got to Blairlogie? My gloomy view of the passing countryside was punctuated by the occasional self-pitying sob. Not very far from the village, Bella came and sat beside me.

"I'm no' goin' t'say anything about this, but if y'do it again, I will. Understand?" I nodded glumly. "Good! It's forgotten then. *He* has."

Charlie was kneeling on his seat, singing happily to himself as he gazed out of the window.

Footnote: Not all that long after this episode, but quite unrelated to it I assure you, the Allans moved back to the family farm in Aberdeenshire. Charles Allan, as many of you will know, grew up to be a real lad o' pairts – farmer, lecturer on things agricultural, journalist, writer, folk-singer, wit, raconteur *and* world-champion caber-tosser. Quite!

Blairlogie Kirk

It's small, it's plain and, along with the rest of the village, it sits snugly in the shelter of the rocky outcrops of Castle Law and Goats' Craig above. Its very existence is a legacy of the struggles, splits and upheavals that characterised the Church of Scotland in the eighteenth and nineteenth centuries – a complex series of events warranting just a wee bit of historical background.

With the twin thorns of Episcopacy and patronage removed and Presbyterianism fully in control as a result of the Revolution Settlement of 1690, the Kirk's future augured well; the more so when William and Mary's adviser on things Scottish, William Carstares, became both Principal of Edinburgh University and leader of the Church of Scotland. A shrewd and subtle politician, Carstares could appear sympathetic to the extremists of whom there were many and, at the same time, devise ways of controlling and guiding them as he saw fit. Within the space of eight years, however, three events conspired to upset the Kirk's unaccustomed stability.

The first of these was the bitterly resented but inevitable Union of Parliaments in 1707. While this didn't affect the Church of Scotland directly, the Act of Union exposed it to the influence of political intrigue as the second event proved.

With Anne (daughter of James II & VII) on the throne, some of the Kirk's old anxieties anent relations with the House of Stewart must have been close to resurfacing; they did in 1712 when her parliament passed an act restoring the hated system of patronage which took the right to call a minister out of the hands of the congregation and placed it in those of the heritors – local landowners and proprietors.

The final blow came in 1715 with the death of William Carstares and, with it, the realisation that the spiritual tide which had flowed so strongly and widely since 1690 was, in some quarters, on the ebb. With Carstares' strong leadership gone, that which he had so assiduously held together began to fall apart and two distinct religious positions emerged; one was occupied by the unwaveringly dogmatic Calvinists (the Evangelicals) while the other attracted those of a more tolerant, less confrontational persuasion (the Moderates).

Moderate ministers held many of the university chairs of the time and there were always plenty of professors in the General Assembly, so it was no great surprise when this group also assumed leadership of the Kirk; a boon, incidentally, for that great burst of intellectual activity later in the eighteenth century – the Scottish Enlightenment. And so, with the Evangelicals objecting to the high-handed and less than fervent attitude of the Moderates, the scene was set for the first breakaway.

In 1733, Ebenezer Erskine and his associates formed the United Secession Church to be followed by the foundation of the Relief Church in 1761 – a splinter group led by Thomas Gillespie and his supporters. (It was at this point that Blairlogie Kirk came into being.) Secession and Relief eventually joined forces and resources in 1847 to become the United Presbyterian Church.

The big one, of course, came in 1843 when not far short of half the clergy, including the Moderator, walked out of the General Assembly of the Church of Scotland and formed the Free Church of Scotland.

In 1900, the United Presbyterian and Free Church, minus a minority of the latter who continued to be known by that name, joined to form the United Free Church and, in 1929, the United Free, minus another minority who, again, continued to be known by that name, rejoined the Church of Scotland.

And so, after virtually two hundred years of vigorous soul-searching during which the Church of Scotland rent itself asunder, it nearly all came together again; nearly, but not quite. The rumps comprising the United Free Church (*not* the Wee Frees) and the Free Church (the Wee Frees) remained independent along with some tiny splinter groups such as the Free Presbyterians, the United Original Seceders and the Reformed Presbyterians. The latter, incidentally, descended directly from the Cameronians who, refusing to sign up to the Revolution Settlement of 1690 on the grounds that it did not go far enough, had remained determinedly aloof from any so-called Church of Scotland. It's little wonder, then, that Scottish towns of quite modest proportions can contain a clutch of church buildings of the various Presbyterian strains. It's also little wonder that so many of them are either redundant or poorly used.

What then of Blairlogie Kirk? Well, it was born of the old Logie Kirk, so we must start there.

Alexander Douglas was minister from 1688 until his death in 1720, a period which neatly covered events already referred to – especially the 1712 restoration of patronage. Trouble erupted when he died. For two years no successor was appointed as Session and congregation steadfastly refused to accept the various nominees of the heritors. A split loomed but was, in fact, averted when Patrick Duchal was presented for his trial preaching. He so impressed his listeners that they readily agreed to his appointment – heritor nominated or no. For the following thirty-six years, equanimity reigned in Logie Parish under the benign guidance and leadership of this good man. Indeed, so resolutely were Session and congregation behind their minister that they saw off a pretty determined group of Ebenezer Erskine's supporters who were actively seeking recruits to join their seceding movement. An account of this confrontation is given in a pamphlet published in 1739 and splendidly entitled 'The Fatal and Lamentable End of Mr Ebenezer's Artificial Tabernacle in its Perigrination (*sic*) to Logie.' The tabernacle in question

The old Manse in middle distance. First Blairlogie post office right foreground. c.1860.

The Manse as it looks today. c. 1960.

was an elaborate and substantial tent in which the seceders held their meetings – their days of 'Fasting and Humiliation' as they called them. It would appear that the ensuing scuffle, during which much intemperate language was identified, culminated in the breaking of the tabernacle and the resolve of the seceders. They fled the field.

Patrick Duchal died in 1758 and so did the long period of peace and harmony which had characterised his incumbency. There now followed three years of bitter dissent and intransigence which ended with Logie congregation splitting in two very unequal parts.

The Earl of Dunmore's determination to establish himself as heid-heritor, as it were, led directly to this unhappy state of affairs. His first nominee, realising he was on a hiding to nothing, wisely sought and was offered a living elsewhere. Clearly a heritor's man he harangued the Session and congregation in a letter to the Presbytery of Dunblane which concluded... "[they] have betrayed an unchristian spirit, I pity them, I pray for them and I quit them with pleasure." The Earl's next nominee was one James Wright and, at this point, heels were ever more deeply dug in and complete impasse was reached. Dunmore refused to budge and, indeed, forced the appointment through at which the entire Kirk Session, save one, walked out with the books and the great majority of the members.

Having taken this first, momentous step, the new congregation didn't hang about; funding was raised and work started on the construction of a church in Blairlogie; application was made to join the newly formed Presbytery of Relief and, through that agency, it was not long before they had their own minister. Indeed, by 1762 they had achieved all three.

Prior to completion of the new church, services were held on the hillside at the back of Blairlogie Castle; the preaching stone can still be seen on the flat part of what is a grassy, natural auditorium. Of course the weather didn't always look favourably on this brave new enterprise; on the occasions when shelter was required, a tent was pitched – probably on the land adjacent

The original Blairlogie Kirk (burned down in 1845)
and Manse (pulled down in 1864)

from a sketch dated 1843

As described

Manse and Kirk Mark 2. The former is now a private house.

to Montana Cottage at the top of the village. The inadequacy and additional cost of this arrangement could well have acted as a spur to complete the building work speedily.

All that was needed now was somewhere to house Rev. John Warden (the first minister) and those who would come after him; in 1765, an honest, seemly two-storey Manse was built, complementing perfectly a small, country Kirk.

What today's visitor sees is Kirk and Manse Mark 2 for, in 1845, the former was all but destroyed by fire and, in 1864, the latter was demolished to make way for the present building.

A sketch (*q.v.*) dated 1843 shows a very different window and door arrangement from that found in today's Kirk. The artist was sitting to the south of the building, looking north and I'm inclined to think there's been a change of axis. Today, the pulpit is against the west wall and pews, placed on either side of a central aisle, face it. Looking at the contemporary sketch, it seems to me highly likely that the pulpit would have been against the south wall – in front of the two smaller and central windows – with pews facing it from the three remaining walls. In pre-amplification days, this axis would have made more acoustical sense. It is known that there was a gallery which ran along the north wall; judging by the tiny window on the left of the façade, it may also have extended along the west and east walls. All this extra seating was essential because, at the time of its building, the Relief Kirk was the only one of its denomination for miles around and the large congregation walked from as far afield as Alva, Tullibody and Bridge of Allan as well as nearer to home.

And what of the fire? Rev. Robert Anderson (minister number seven [1885-1921]) describes it thus in his excellent little book '150 Years in Blairlogie'...

> In November of that year [1845], on a cold, frosty morning, the heating apparatus was called upon for extra duty and responded with the result that the venerable fabric, built in 1761, was well nigh destroyed. Nothing remained of the wooden fixtures; only a few movable seats were rescued and the lower half of the walls. There are still with us a few who remember the sad conflagration. [**Anderson's book was written in 1912**.] Several who attended the Parish Church of Logie

gave valuable assistance in carrying pails of water to extinguish the burning pile, but the seats were over 80 years old, and lent rapidly to the devouring flame.

After an initial despair, sleeves were rolled up and, on August 16, 1846 – ten months later – the new church opened its doors for worship. By now, of course, the Blairlogie congregation was considerably smaller; the Disruption of 1843, and with it the building of new dissenting churches all over the place, saw to that. Although rebuilt on what was left of the walls, fewer sittings were needed which meant that the gallery could be dispensed with, the roof could, therefore, be lower and, as described above, the axis changed; all of which led to sittings for a congregation of about two hundred and forty.

Time for a tiny digression. As a child, I used to wonder why there were no windows in the north wall; actually, their absence provided a splendid surface against which to practise the ball skills essential to a member of the future Blairlogie Thistle, so I wasn't too concerned. The answer to my childish pondering had to be that **a)** the heating source for the rebuilt church was in the same position as before; central to the north wall with the chimney equally central above it – *not* where it is now and **b)** much of that wall must have been relatively undamaged by the fire. This came to light in the 1970s, I think, when the wall was being re-harled and, in the process, the old entrance to the former gallery was discovered complete with a lower pair of door-hinge pins but no upper ones; an indication, surely, that the entrance and, therefore, the roof must have been higher than it at present appears. Anyway, it was decided to make a feature of this direct link with the past, so it is *not* a blocked up window; it is part of a blocked up door. Access to the latter would have been by means of a broad, wooden stairway, presumably with a handrail of some sort.

The thinking behind the demolition of the first Manse is hard to fathom; I can't believe there was anything structurally wrong with it because it was seven or eight years *younger* than our own house which is still going strong. I think it was nothing more than a piece of Victorian ostentation with a heavy hint of snobbery thrown in. Clearly Rev. William McLaren (minister number six [1851 – 1884]) and the Kirk Session felt that the douce, whitewashed and simple building lacked dignity or status or something. In other words, it looked like too many other houses in the village. For whatever reason, it was razed to the ground and the present ponderous Victorian villa raised in its place. To quote Robert Anderson again ...

> In the year 1864 steps were taken to build a new Manse in place of the old one, which had done duty for over 100 years. The present elegant and commodious Manse was built on the site of the old one.

Commodious certainly, but elegant? I wonder.

When we came to live in Blairlogie, the incumbent was Rev. John McDonald (minister number eight[1921-1951]), an islander from Benbecula whose first language was Gaelic in which he did all his preparatory work before translating it into the English for the benefit of his lowland congregation. A bachelor, he and his elderly house-keeper, Miss Shepherd, stotted around the vastness of the Manse like two lonely peas in a huge pod. Her sphere of influence was the kitchen, the outer offices and the tiniest bedroom imaginable; his was the rest – there was a lot of it.

In common with many others, John McDonald decided to take his congregation back into the fold of the Church of Scotland in 1929 – a move which went against the wishes of the great majority, but, reluctantly, the flock followed its Shepherd (minister, not house-keeper). Indeed, only one member actually left because of McDonald's decision. And so in the space of one hundred and sixty eight years, Blairlogie's wee Kirk experienced four denominations – Relief, U.P., U.F. and C. of S.; it was assumed the last would be just that. Not so.

John McDonald's health, which for some time had been poor, finally led to an early retirement. Claiming a shortage of ministers, thus making it difficult to fill the vacancy, the Church of Scotland wasted no time in recommending union with either Menstrie or Logie. Inevitably, this course would

Rev R. F. Anderson (right) author of "150 years in Blairlogie", his sistser Jane who acted housekeeper 'til he got married and brother George, an Edinburgh lawyer, c. 1890.

have led to our eventual closure so we refused and suggested instead a linkage with one or the other; *they* refused and impasse existed again. Negotiations went on for a couple of years achieving absolutely nothing. A point was reached where those of the congregation who were pro-C. of S. (about ten) worshipped in the Kirk while the antis (about sixty) held Sunday services in the Reading Room; church door locks were changed and changed again – the whole thing was grist to a journalistic mill and, ever keen to highlight squabbles among the 'holy', the papers had a wonderful time.

An application to rejoin the U.F. Church was narrowly turned down; clearly some mistrusted our motives so we did what had been done a hundred and ninety two years before – we seceded. This time we were entirely on our own – no cosy Presbytery of Relief to give us shelter. Our isolation was mercifully short lived though; at a second time of asking, the U.F. Church re-admitted us in late 1953 and we're still together. It's now a link-charge – with Moncrieff U.F. in Alloa – but Blairlogie's wee Kirk still functions and will, hopefully, so continue – *D.V.*!

The War

The war, and all its horrors, touched me little, protected as I was by a combination of childish insouciance and the fact that Blairlogie was not high on any enemy hit-list. Nevertheless, I sometimes found evidence of it inescapable.

My daily bus journey to school passed a camp housing Italian prisoners of war; I was fascinated by it. The internees wore chocolate-brown battledress with big, yellow discs of material stitched on to the blouse backs and smaller ones on the trousers; many of them congregated by the fence beside the road to wave at any passing vehicle, but it was what they had done within the camp ground that held the attention of all but the cynical in our bus. A previously featureless field, just before Devon Village on the Tillycoultry-Alloa road, had been transformed, with typical Mediterranean flair, into a veritable patchwork of white-stone bordered flower beds, paths and plots featuring miniature windmills, churches, houses and all sorts. This was a place of magic and I was delighted to wave back to the seemingly cheery chaps on the other side of the fence. That they were not all cheery chaps was revealed in a report in the Stirling Journal of 8th October, 1942 – noted when I was looking for something else.

SWASTIKA IN SCOTTISH TOWN
Coalman Stops Lorryload of Italians.
A coal merchant in a Central Scottish town figured in an incident with a lorryload of Italian prisoners of war at the end of last week, when he stopped the lorry and protested against the presence of a

> swastika painted by the prisoners on a tea box. The prisoners are conveyed to the farms and back to their camp by means of a covered lorry, at the rear of which they usually congregate singing Italian songs, shouting, "Duce! Duce!" or "Garibaldi" and making fun of the 'V' sign. Recently they have painted the swastika and the Italian flag on a large tea chest which they use as a seat.
>
> As the Italians' lorry approached the driver got out of his own lorry and signalled to the other driver to stop. Then he made an effort to pull down the swastika emblem, but the 30 Italians jumped out and surrounded him. The coal merchant pushed his way back to his own vehicle, but when he armed himself with a stick and turned round to re-enter the fray he saw that the Italians had scrambled into their lorry which was then driven quickly away.

I like it! A fine, bold fellow thon coalman and, clearly, not one to argue with.

The habit of using prisoners of war on the land became even more widespread as the conflict progressed. When its end was in sight, German POWs of a suitably demure demeanour were also used in this capacity – and not just on farms. My mother applied for, and was granted, POW assistance with our, then, postage stamp of a garden. So, on three consecutive days at the war's end, a lorry deposited a German warrior at our front door in the morning and picked him up in the evening; all my mother had to do was give him tools and midday sustenance.

The language barrier was enormous. Mother's German consisted of musical terms, none of which proved remotely applicable to gardening and the warrior's English didn't exist at all. One word dominated their attempts at communication – *kaput!* Most of the plants in our little garden, particularly those mother indicated she wished left alone, were dismissed as *kaput*; the tools he was given were *kaput* (this was probably quite accurate, father having found them on some tip or other); the weather was *kaput*; *everything* was *kaput*. At the end of his three day assault, the former green and friendly little jungle had been reduced to bare earth with, here and there, an isolated and deeply shocked plant clinging desperately to the exposed soil.

On his last day, mother had to go to a rehearsal in Glasgow, so I was charged with providing his midday repast. To that end, she had emptied a tin of tomato soup into a covered pan and all I had to do was heat it, transfer the contents into a plate, take the protective cloth off another plate with a hunk of bread on it and carry a tray bearing this culinary creation to the poor man.

Deeply suspicious of this German killing-machine, I enlisted the company of Mossie – possibly so that in the event of one of us being attacked, the other could effect an escape and alert the village. That seemed to be the thinking. Having not the least idea how long it might take to heat the soup, but remembering that I mustn't let it boil, the pan was whipped off the cooker at the very first wisp of steam.

We carried the tray out to the would-be conqueror and stood at a respectful distance while he stirred the contents of the plate thoughtfully before transferring a spoonful to his mouth. Wide-eyed and slack-jawed we watched a jet of virtually cold tomato soup hit the ground at speed, closely followed by a stream of funny sounding words, the clearest and loudest of which was *KAPUT!* He had his revenge though. Apparently, every root exposed in the digging process had been ruthlessly chopped into many little bits, each of which produced its own growth. By the following season, the jungle at Kirklea Cottage had returned greener, lusher and denser than ever it had been. A late victory for the *Wehrmacht* but I think my mother, secretly, was rather relieved.

* * *

After Dunkirk, when Britain stood wounded and pretty much alone, the Government hit on the idea of appealing to the population at large for the desperately needed money to rebuild and rearm our shattered forces. This was to be money over and above anything generated by income tax; it was a Governmental begging-bowl held out in the direction of patriotic pockets, purses and wallets. Each year, one week was set aside nationally to allow every county and its constituent cities, towns, villages and districts to squeeze as much money as possible out of its populace. By giving each collecting week a title and cleverly setting every collecting area a target, it really was a most successful enterprise. 1941 was 'War Weapons Week'; 1942 – 'Warship Week'; 1943 – 'Wings for Victory Week' and 1944 – 'Salute the Soldier Week'. Of course, even patriotism could be persuaded to part with more if it was getting something for its money, so each collecting week was filled with all kinds of events from plain old can-rattling and the like to dances, parades, competitions, concerts – anything that would generate enough cash to enable a collecting committee to meet its target. Blairlogie was very much a part of the scheme and the money it raised on these occasions was truly remarkable.

Obviously, the area being tapped was 'Greater' Blairlogie – the surrounding farms, hamlets and houses as well as the village itself. Total population? Two hundred and fifty at the outside (and I don't really think it was anything like that). This wee community was, in 1944, set a collecting target of £2,500 for the week – ten pounds for every man, woman and child if my population over-estimate is accepted; more if it isn't. Now remember, apart from two or three 'Big Houses' with, perhaps, biggish money and a clutch of middle-class households where there might have been a bit to spare, this was, overwhelmingly, an area of farming, mining and labouring families. And what was a working-wage then? Four pounds a week? Maybe not even that. For 'Salute the Soldier Week' of 1944, this tiny community raised £7,020 – £28 per man, woman and child. I find that quite amazing.

* * *

My own experience of wartime deprivation amounted to managing my weekly sugar ration. This was not easy because I was very partial to the stuff – rather a lot of it. That had been my undoing. Mother, incensed at the sight of me ladling it on to my breakfast cereal one morning, decided, there and then, to correct my errant way. My share of sugar was put in a bowl – just for me – and I was told I could do with it as I wished – use it all up at once or learn to spread it over the week. Because she was my mother and I reckoned she was only kidding, I chose the former and was immediately mortified to discover she was very serious – no more sugar 'til next week. Gnashing of teeth and wails of tearful remorse failed to change her mind. Small boys learn big lessons the hard way.

For the adult, exposed to wartime anxieties, restrictions and shortages on a daily basis, times must have been depressingly difficult; any opportunity to get out of the rut of drab existence, however briefly, was gratefully taken. An escape was provided by radio and the cinema, but the latter wasn't always easy to reach if you lived out in the country. Of course, if the entertainment could come to you...

In 1940, father put on a radio revue from the Glasgow studios called 'Lights Up'. The cast, which comprised Madeline Christie, C.R.M. (Charlie) Brookes, Mollie Weir, Janet Brown, Edith Stevenson and my mother, acted, sang, played and did their own sound effects – all with great gusto. With an augmented cast (Nan Scott, Willie Joss, Jimmy Urquhart, Grace McChlery and Alec Ross were the extras) father put it on at Glasgow's Lyric Theatre for the entertainment of citizenry and armed forces alike. Then he had the brainwave of taking the smaller cast version of the show to those who lived, or were stationed, far away from a big centre like Glasgow; all that was needed was a stage, a piano and, if possible (but not essential), a bright light or two. Most village halls could manage that – Blairlogie's Reading Room certainly could. In her book, 'A Toe on the Ladder', Mollie Weir describes some of the logistic difficulties involved...

> That was only the first of many shows we did for the troops. Moultrie and Ruby organised them, and we did shows under various titles, like 'Salute the Soldier' concerts, 'Prisoner of War' entertainments, 'Salute to the Navy' shows. We ranged quite far afield, and when Stirlingshire seemed a good central base for our week-end activities, we stayed in Moultrie's lovely house in Blairlogie. ... The feeling of being in real country was a benison in itself, after the dark pressures of Glasgow

tenements, when the drone of bombers conjured thoughts of tons of masonry on top of us. In the country, the stars shone comfortingly and all that beautiful untenanted space was a solace to the mind.

But it was really quite a small house, although it seemed large to me after tenement life, and we all had to double up for sleeping accommodation, and I found myself one night with Madeline Christie. I was snug as a bug, but at breakfast time she stared at me accusingly. "I will never share a bed with that one again", she said, "I've spent my married life training my husband never to put his feet near mine. I can't *bear* people's feet. And now I've had the misery of pursuing feet chasing mine all night."

...Mollie thought she was joking, but Aunt Madeline, who could be the haughty one when she chose, was very serious.

With only two bedrooms, the house was small all right; the women had the beds and the men made do with sleeping-bags on the sitting-room floor. Obviously, my room was commandeered, but that was fine by me because it meant that I would be sleeping at Berryholes – a farmlet a few hundred yards west of Blairlogie where lived Kate Gilmour who 'did' for mother a lot of the time. Here, at close quarters, I could study a cow, a pig, hens and I would be fed mince on toast. Never tried it? I thought it was great! The only downside to this, otherwise, perfect arrangement was the earth-closet; I wasn't at all keen on that and would go to considerable, and sometimes uncomfortable, lengths to avoid using it.

If the two or three times they played in Blairlogie Reading Room were anything to go by, it was a most successful venture. Don't ask me how they coped with travel and petrol problems – I haven't a clue – but there was always a way round these little difficulties during the war.

* * *

Death and injury, or the prospect of either, was a concept that did not exercise us greatly. Our only experience of both was gleaned from cowboy films in which men and horses constantly crashed to the ground in large numbers, either to lie still or writhe in apparent agony, as the white-hats (goodies) consigned the black-hats (baddies) to eating dirt yet again. A favourite white-hat – certainly mine – was Hopalong Cassidy. A bit on the short side for a hero and with a gammy leg – hence the nickname – he was seldom separated from his horse. In the event of the story-line requiring that he should be dismounted, movement was kept to a minimum and he sported a rather tall white stetson to increase his less than heroic proportions. To a lesser degree, we went along with Gene Autrey, but Roy Rogers was scorned – after all, he played guitar and sang to his horse. What kind of a cowboy was that, for goodness' sake! Having been parentally assured that, once the camera was switched off, *all* the bodies got up again, the mayhem on screen was viewed without any feelings of horror and revulsion – it was fun, and we could cheer white-hat safe in the knowledge that black-hat and his horse were only acting. This was bad preparation for reality – especially when there was a war on – and reality duly visited Blairlogie on 30th April, 1944.

As one would expect, there was a clearly defined order of precedence among the young of the village. Top dogs at the time were those of fifteen, sixteen and over – men as far as we (at eight, nine and ten-ish) of the second tier were concerned; and then came those at the bottom of this pile of boys – the wee pains, the ones who always got in your way; exactly how the top dogs viewed *us*. Anyway, two from the top, along with a couple of slightly younger Menstrie lads, went for a walk on Sunday, 30th April – a walk towards disaster. The Stirling Journal of 4th May, 1944 gave this typically flat, factual account...

PICKED UP OBJECT
YOUTH KILLED AND COMPANION INJURED.

A 16-year-old boy was killed and [his] 15-year-old companion seriously injured while out on a bird-nesting expedition on the Sheriffmuir, near Stirling, on Sunday. It appears that the elder boy picked up a rusty object and had thrown it at a stone, and that the object had exploded.

James Millar (16), farm servant, Cotkerse, Blairlogie and William

Russell (15), apprentice baker, Blair House, Blairlogie were in company with two Menstrie schoolboys – Archibald Harkins (13) and William Hunter (12).

Near a wood Millar picked up a rusty object, announcing that he was going to throw it at a stone. The schoolboys, thinking the object resembled a bomb, ran away, but they had not gone far when they heard an explosion. Afraid to go back to the spot, they went home and made no mention of what had occurred.
About seven hours later, it is understood, Russell arrived at his home between two and three miles from the scene of the accident, in an exhausted condition, suffering from injuries to his neck, right arm and right thigh. He was later removed to Stirling Royal Infirmary.

When he told what had occurred, a search party was organised for Millar of whom nothing had been heard. It was not until after two o'clock on Monday morning that his body was found on the moor by Mr George Jeffrey of St Andrew's Ambulance Association who was a member of the search party.

Millar had been badly injured about the forehead and Dr Gordon, Alva, who was a member of the search party, was of the opinion that he had been dead for some hours.

A piece of shrapnel was found in Russell's neck when he was examined at the infirmary, and this has been successfully removed.

The schoolboys explained that why they left the scene before the explosion occurred was that they recognised the object as one of the "Don't Touch" things illustrated on a poster they had seen at school.

What this bland piece of reportage couldn't convey – the pain, the panic, the loneliness – was, to some extent, revealed at the enquiry a couple of months later.

Unwittingly, the quartet had stumbled on a military shooting range though there was no indication of this – it wasn't cordoned off in any way and there were no warning signs. Indeed, it was only after the explosion that Willie Russell had noticed a nearby target consisting of three barrels.

After Jimmy Millar had picked up what was later identified as a Smith Gun high explosive shell and shown it to the others, Willie had turned away at which Jimmy must have thrown it down. As Willie told the enquiry, he was struck on the neck and thigh and fell to the ground. The boys from Menstrie had already taken off, and though he tried to call them back to help, he couldn't speak properly and passed out.

When he came to, he crawled towards Jimmy who was lying on his back. Willie asked him if he could make it to the Sheriffmuir Road and though he couldn't answer, he struggled to his feet and they walked a few yards (over difficult terrain, remember) before collapsing again. Jimmy lost consciousness.

Because his arm had also been damaged, Willie couldn't lift him and, after failing to attract the attention of some distant people, he waited for Jimmy to regain consciousness. He didn't. Painfully and very slowly, Willie made for home.

This particular range was allotted to local Home Guard units, one of which had last used the area on 9th April – three weeks before this tragedy. An officer admitted at the enquiry that, while every endeavour was made to locate and collect unexploded shells, it was not always possible to do so. Constable Gordon of Causewayhead, who was leading the search-party, actually found another unexploded and similar shell a mere twenty five feet from poor Jimmy's pool of blood. If they knew that live ammunition was lying around, it seems incredible that *no* warning/danger signs were erected. This wasn't even commented on by the Sheriff who, in his summing up, laid the onus on others.

> "...How this shell came to be there is inexplicable, but these things do happen when there is a war going on. What I would hope is that this sad accident will again remind all parents and teachers to impress on all their boys not to touch any suspicious or unknown objects they may find."

The Home Guard was whitewashed!

Jimmy had been killed, Willie was in Stirling Royal Infirmary for three weeks and Blairlogie was in a state of shock – mourning for the dead and the damaged and fearful lest any of its other bairns should experience a similar fate. But the dreadful message had got through to us; indeed, it wasn't until quite a few years after the war that we even considered leaving the safety of Sheriffmuir's road to strike out across the heather.

* * *

With Japan atom bombed into submission, the Second World War finally came to an end on 14th August, 1945; now the celebrations could really begin. Those village adults inclined to discuss such things were of the opinion that Blairlogie's contribution to this nation-wide orgy of relief should take the form of something-for-the-bairns – a treat of some sort, but just *what* sort was, as yet, unclear. It would require money and raising this would require time so, with summer all but over, it seemed best to take a long term view and plan something for the following year. And that's what happened; fourteen well-meaning souls formed a committee to organise the Blairlogie District Children's Victory Treat, as it was rather ponderously called. Tellingly, the fourteen comprised a home-sharing brother and sister and six married couples; of the latter, four were childless – a moderately significant statistic.

The first of thirteen meetings took place on 24th January, 1946 but it was clear that some thought had already been given to the event; the Minute book reveals talk of 'Badges and Brooches' quite early on; it seemed that part of the treat was to be a memento in the shape of a badge (boys) or brooch (girls) depicting a view of part of the village – this rather out-of-touch decision reflected the committee's composition.

Social events were to be the mainstay of fund-raising and, to that end, a whist-drive (tickets 2/6) and dance (tickets 1/6) in the Reading Room was scheduled for the evening of 15th February. The Minute book reveals two nice little pointers to social attitudes in those days. It was arranged that a cup of tea should be provided for the dancers at the interval and Messrs Miller, Harvey and Miss Allan, musicians all, offered their services for *nothing*. Actually the committee, impressed by this generous gesture, voted in favour of giving each a small gift of cigarettes. The image of a Miss Allan being slipped 20 Woodbine, or whatever, is a nice one.

After paying a couple of bills – 5/- for the hire of 20 tables and 56 chairs and 4/- to hire crockery and an urn – the profit realised was over £46 and the committee was well pleased; indeed, they resolved to repeat the exercise but without the whist-drive element. Messrs Miller, Harvey and Miss Allan again volunteered their services free of charge but they indicated that they would like the assistance of an accordionist, but *he* wasn't prepared to do anything for nothing – he wanted a fee! The committee didn't demur and it was all arranged for 5th April from 7.45pm to 2.00am. Not quite so successful this one – only £20.11.10d. Still, the bank balance now stood at £67.17.10d which was deemed more than satisfactory.

In March, 1946, the government intimated that Saturday, 8th June was to be a day of national victory celebrations, so that became the BDCVT committee's goal but, about this time, the first indication of disagreement within this august body was revealed and it centred on the brooches; for reasons of economy, the idea of badges had been dropped – boys, as well as girls, were to be given brooches. Yes, that's what *I* thought!

The artistic Miss Crum (of the brother/sister couple) had designed this and, of its kind, it was very good; I wish, now, I still had mine. But to give a brooch to a boy, especially one who could be anything up to sixteen, was a bit daft. The real area of conflict, however, was that of entitlement – who was to get one. Some on the committee wanted every child to have one, others said only those who had been resident in the village up to VJ-day should be recipients; in other words, incomers were oot so to speak. The final arrangement was that those few children who had arrived in the district *after* VJ-day would receive a peace badge – cheaper and readily available nationally. A divisive decision if ever there was one. Our brooches, incidentally, were costing 7/6 each to manufacture. I'd rather have had the money.

The date of the treat was due to clash with entertainments being run by schools in the area, so it was changed to 22nd June and the final programme was to include a fancy dress and decorated cycle parade, sports (prizes 1/-, 6d and 3d for 1st, 2nd and 3rd), a conjuror, ice-cream and, in the evening, a dance for the grownups – music provided by Messrs Miller, Gray and Rennie. Change of personnel here. Presumably Mr Harvey and Miss Allan had overdosed on Woodbine.

The Stirling Observer of 25th June,1946 describes the occasion thus...

CHILDREN'S TREAT

The committee of the Blairlogie and District Children's Treat Fund brought their labours to a successful and enjoyable climax on Saturday when the children were entertained to a varied sports programme in a field on Blairmains Farm, kindly lent by Mr John Eadie. Ices were served and later the children sat down to tea in the Reading Room.

Each child who had resided in the district during the war years was presented with a most attractive brooch depicting a view of Blairlogie village, carried out in enamel, which had been designed by Miss Crum of Gogar. Children who had come to the district since the termination of the war were presented with peace medals. Miss Crum, who made the presentations, gave the children a most inspiring address. Thereafter Mr James Bruce, Stirling, delighted everyone with his conjuring tricks.

On Friday evening a fancy dress parade was held for the children who turned out in most attractive and original costumes. The entrants met in The Square, paraded to Cotkerse headed by pipers Oliver and Drummond in Highland dress, and thence to Blairmains Farm where Mr George J. Sherriff, county clerk of Stirlingshire, judged the costumes. Mrs Sherriff presented the prizes, and before disbanding Mrs Eadie generously provided the children with refreshments. Prize-winners at the fancy dress parade were:-

Tiny tots – 1(equal), Jean Loudon (Red Cross Nurse) and Jim Loudon (Student); 2(equal) Robert Russell (Wee Willie Winkie) and Annie Muir (Little Red Riding Hood).

Non-Cycle Class – Girls – Most Attractive:- 1, Margaret Oliver (Victorian Lady); 2, Betty Irvine (Gypsy); 3, Eleanor Kay (Dutch Girl).

Non-Cycle Class – Boys – 1, Ian Kay (Tattie Bogle); 2, John Eadie (Sacked).

Most Original – 1, Douglas Evans (Minister); 2, Jim Smith (Onion Boy).
Cycle Class – Girls -1, Elspeth McLeish (Dutch Girl); 2, Jean Miller (Dutch Girl). – Boys – 1, Robin Kelsall (Mufti); 2, David McLeish (Cowboy).
Consolation – Hugh Muir (Flower Cycle).

To conclude the celebrations the committee held a most enjoyable dance in the Reading Room on Saturday evening, excellent music being provided by Mr D. Gray, Causewayhead.

No, I never wore my brooch – certainly not in public – and I probably contrived to lose it as soon as possible. Something I now regret.

Rear (l. to r.): R. Kelsall; E. McLeish; D. Evans; J. Miller.
Centre (l. to r.): B. Irvine; M. Oliver; D. McLeish; I. Kay; J. Eadie; J. Smith; E. Kay.
Front (l. to r.): J. Loudon; J. Loudon; A. Muir.

Gang Warfare

I suppose we numbered about six or seven and probably ranged in age from nine to twelve. Whatever the statistics, the fact remains that, as a fighting unit, the Blairlogie gang struck fear into the hearts of no one – least of all our perceived enemy, the numerically superior Menstrie gang. Our tactics were minimal; if outnumbered, the normal state of affairs, run; if numerical advantage lay with us – it happened once – make the most of it. In short, our gang was at its best when there was not the slightest chance of confrontation.

Organisation was our strong point; we held meetings in a room of one of the row of derelict cottages in Victoria Place, laying plans to deal with scenarios we fervently hoped would never arise; we posted a look-out in the big, old pear tree behind the cottages. Being surrounded by buildings, this was a singularly useless ploy; by the time whoever was on duty espied the enemy, they'd be milling around the foot of the tree chucking things at him. Bizarrely, we awarded each other decorations. Let me explain.

Papers and cinema newsreels of the time were full of heroically beribboned soldiery of one rank or another; these medal-ribbons caught my eye and imagination. With the aid of a roll of sticky white tape, utility-standard coloured pencils and some scissors, I devised row upon row of ribbons which we solemnly stuck upon each other's shirt breast. Since the materials were provided by me and, unwittingly, my mother, I had rather more than anyone else.

Our role was purely defensive – a kind of junior Home Guard I suppose – for even in our wildest imagination, we never saw ourselves taking on the might of Menstrie on its home ground. Indeed, it was a place to be avoided whenever possible. The whining that greeted a maternal request to fetch thence some 'message' unobtainable at Blairlogie's shop could reach quite dramatic proportions; only the threat of instant house arrest for the remainder of the day cut through the shrill complaints. Having acquiesced gracelessly, the next thing was to enlist company for the bike dash there and back. This was deemed the best means of slipping into, and out of, enemy territory because **a)** vigorously pedalled machines are awkward to stop and hard to hit, **b)** an extra pair of eyes and, in the last resort, fists was useful and **c)** it was a comfort to have someone guarding the bikes while the purchase was being made. Experience had shown that although the bus took you further into the village, thus cutting exposure to hostile elements, there was no guarantee that there might be an adult (preferably *several* adults) with whom you could pretend an association while anxiously awaiting the bus home. The third way of getting there, on foot, was plainly suicidal.

So what brought the Menstrie battalions to Blairlogie? The extensive orchard on the western edge of the village was the big attraction; at the war's end, it was younger and rather more prolific than now. Before the fruit was really ripe, the enemy infantry used to appear armed with sticks to dislodge the booty and bags to put it in. From the strip of woodland which, in those days, ran alongside the main road and separated it from the orchard, they would fan out, two or three to a tree; one knocked off the lower fruit with his stick, another swarmed in among the branches shaking and stamping on them to free their bounty and there might be yet another to bag it all.

And what of the highly decorated junior Home Guard? Keeping out of sight mainly; an occasional fusillade of green apples in the general direction of the marauders was about the sum total of our defiance. Of course, if we could draw the attention of a concerned grown-up to the pilfering, that was another matter. In those days, the adult voice – especially an indignant male one – was heeded and a righteous roar suggesting speedy departure elicited a most satisfactory response; bodies tumbled out of trees, bags were grabbed and sticks abandoned amid a general stampede for the cover of the roadside wood.

The sheer waste that characterised such forays littered the raiders' route home; unripe apples, pears and plums with one mouth-twisting bite out of them lay where they'd been hurled in disgust. We were just as bad, for childhood is often an impatient and selfish state – always fearful of missing out on something; whether it's fruit, chestnuts or whatever, if it looks big enough it'll do and, besides, when it's in *your* pocket, it can't be in anyone else's.

One day of late summer when the fruit was approaching its best, something unusual happened. Maybe they were confident of avoiding detection; maybe they wanted to be one up on their pals; maybe they had little or no regard for our ability to see them off; maybe it was a bit of all three. Whatever the reason, two known members of the Menstrie gang were seen browsing among the branches of an apple tree near the roadside wood. Close questioning of our informant confirmed that there was no sign of any others – just the two of them. There could be no hiding place this time; action had to be taken; a lesson had to be taught.

A frontal assault was out of the question; they, being in the tree, had the advantage of height and a goodly supply of apple-ammo to hand. No, this called for one of our carefully planned but untested ambushes.

<u>Chosen site</u> – the wall on either side of the gate to Dougie and Mossie's house (where the entrance to the car-park on the east of the village is today).
<u>Weaponry and equipment</u> – two garden syringes; four buckets of water; two bicycles.
<u>Ambush primer</u> – tip-off to self-appointed defender-of-the-orchard; one noted for his loud, colourful and effective delivery.

Blairlogie from the west. A very young orchard - target of the Menstrie gang many years later - in the foreground, c. 1900.

Ambush springer – tackety boots scuffing the gritty pavement surface; moaning Menstrie mouths.

An out of breath Davie, the tipper-off, and defender-of-the-orchard's bellowed imprecations arrived pretty simultaneously. With about a couple of hundred yards between orchard and ambush, we probably had two or three minutes wait; time for a final test of the quite powerful syringes.

"They're comin'," hoarsely whispered to the team on the far side of the big gate.

"How did thon fat auld bas...?" The querulous query was cut short by a jet of water striking the speaker on the side of the head and ricocheting over his companion. Yelling, the two broke into a run – straight into a well-aimed stream from the other team. In a fit of over-enthusiasm, a bucket of water was added to the effect of the syringe. By now soaked, shocked and squelching, they continued a shambling run towards Menstrie, fumbling desperately for the few apples in their pockets and hurling them defiantly but wildly at their tormentors.

Part two of the plan now fell into place. Recharging their weapons, the syringers leaped on their bikes and pedalled off in pursuit of the hapless quarry; two bucket carriers followed as fast as legs and burden would allow; two others returned to base to replenish water supplies.

And so developed this pattern of bike riders swooping on their demoralised victims, discharging their weapons, returning to bucket carriers, recharging and repeating the sequence. Of *course* it was bullying, but such success had never come our way before so, inevitably, we overdid things.

Normality was restored round about Cotkerse – a couple of hundred yards distant. At this point, the road to Menstrie rises, bends and then falls to a long straight stretch. In other words, you can't see what's coming. Brainwave or bravado surfaced in the bedraggled pair.

"Oor gang's oan its wey an' then we'll come back an' bash yiz," they yelled.

It wasn't and they didn't but we weren't to know this.

Thoughtfully, the syringers brought the news back to the bucketeers who had heard the threat anyway. There was no great debate; truth or no, the bikers were unwilling to pursue the wet ones further. And so the Blairlogie gang's one victory in the field drew to a fairly ignominious end.

We never saw those two again but, by the same token, it was a long time before we went any messages to Menstrie – instant house arrest or no.

Footnote: For their primary schooling these days, the Blairlogie children go to Menstrie, thus mixing with their peers and avoiding the degree of enmity we either experienced or imagined. In the 1940s, the village children travelled to Stirling and, therefore, did not come into social contact with those from Menstrie. Hence the gangs.

Never Again

I don't know how old I was when first I became aware of the habit many grown-ups had of putting a small white tube between their lips and then setting fire to it. Certainly, I couldn't have been much more than ten when five of us decided to conduct a bit of empirical research into this strange pastime.

Our first experiment, in common with many before us, was with sticks of cinnamon. Davie had learned about these in the course of a school playground discussion on things worldly and duly produced some for our delectation; they were treated with appropriate awe. We sat in our hideout, an expanse of mixed thorn bushes whose thick canopy provided shelter against all but the most determined rain, and solemnly lit those flaky, dry twigs. That first and last intake of hot, sickly, blue smoke was expelled with gasping vigour and broken bits of cinnamon as the sticks rapidly disintegrated. Our expressions of disappointed disgust, verbal and facial, suggested **a)** we'd been tricked, **b)** we'd failed to prepare the stuff in some unknown way prior to ignition and **c)** grown-ups didn't smoke it anyway, so we were wasting our time. There and then it was decided that our next bit of research would be with the genuine article – a real cigarette; five preferably.

Getting hold of the things was potentially straightforward; my mother smoked, Davie's father smoked, Dougie and Mossie's mother smoked – there were a lot of them about, but instinct or a tale from a former researcher warned us that pinching them from home was not a good idea. We resolved to buy our own but, since we were not prepared to make an anonymous trip to a shop in the enemy territory of Menstrie, it meant we'd have to make our purchase in Blairlogie's general-store-cum-post-office; subterfuge and detailed planning was essential. After close questioning and discussion, it transpired that only one parent of our little group of status seekers bought fags from the village shop – Dougie and Mossie's mum; the fact that her particular preference was for Craven A tipped meant absolutely nothing to us; a cigarette was a cigarette after all. The advantage of this particular discovery was that it took the pressure off the rest of us; one or both of them would have to buy the things. Clearly if Davie or I went in and asked for ten Craven A for Mrs Evans, suspicious thoughts would begin to stir and surface within the ever watchful proprietrix, Mrs Kennedy. While the rest of us diligently studied things in the burn at the front of the shop, Dougie and Mossie were inside negotiating the deal. The door-bell pinged to indicate its opening and the brothers emerged, slightly red of face, but with the gleam of success in their eyes. Heedful of the fact that Mrs Kennedy could be studying our every move from behind the cluttered window display – goodness knows what she made of the motley collection of farthings, ha'pennies and the odd penny with which our collective purchase was made – we continued to feign interest in the burn while Dougie and Mossie appeared to move purposefully and steadily in the direction of home and Mrs Evans. After what we took to be a decent interval, we joined them round the corner – out of sight of Mrs Kennedy. At speed, we headed for the safety and security of our bushes, hardly able to believe our cunning – ten Craven A; that was two *each*. World of the grown-ups, here we come!

We sat in a circle, each perched on a stone, like a gang of delinquent gnomes, the by now half empty packet lying in the middle. Five cigarettes, held rather too tightly between the first two fingers of five hands, were pressed between five pairs of lips. In unison, we leant towards a solitary flaring match and lit up.

Although we'd studied the smoking technique at length,

clearly one detail had escaped us; grown-ups did not in- and exhale continuously – they had a little rest in between. A thick pall of smoke soon hung heavily in our leafy sanctuary; one by one we stopped our frantic dragging and looked at each other. The glow of healthy boyhood and keen anticipation with which we'd started, had been replaced by a grey-green pallor and glistening beads of perspiration on furrowed brows. The youngest of our bold bunch began to weep quietly; our own feelings of extreme seediness quelled any unpleasant boyish response to his misery and we jerked back in horror when his tears turned into violent retching. That did it. Soggy, half-smoked tabs were ground into the earthen floor along with those left in the packet and we crawled into the open air.

If the grown-ups enjoyed it, they were welcome to it; as far as we were concerned, never again. Unfortunately, that was not so for some of us.

Farm Days

When you're wee and something's three hundred yards away *and* there's a main road between you and that something, even one as comparatively traffic-free as this was, then it might as well be in a foreign land. With the passing of a few years, however, and the acquisition of a modicum of road sense, horizons broaden and so it was that Blairmains eventually came into my ken.

Immediately south of the village, this nineteenth century farm of quite a few acres was, at the time, owned and worked by Jock Eadie who lived in the solidly substantial farmhouse with his wife and their two children, John and Elizabeth.

My introduction to the place was gradual and came through playing with children who already knew something of it. Davie, for instance, once parentally deemed capable of looking after himself and his charge, was dispatched daily to Blairmains with an empty milk-can which he then brought home appropriately filled; I accompanied him from time to time. And, of course, there were the farm-workers' children.

In the angle formed by the junction of Manor Loan with the main road lies a row of whitewashed cottages; these used to house the men who worked on the farm. Condensed into two today, but three at that time, the westernmost was the foreman's; this had an extra room which meant that his accommodation amounted to two rooms with rudimentary kitchen and lavatory. The others, occupied by those of slightly lower status, only provided one room and similarly basic

Jock Eadie with his children John and Elizabeth.

And again, in posing mode.

offices; these tended to change occupants fairly frequently. On the day of a flitting we'd hang around watching arrival or departure with keen interest – sizing up the new or saying goodbye to the old. If the move was local, a horse and trailer did the job; anything further afield called for a lorry. Whatever the transport, family and furniture tended to travel together and often there was as much of the one as the other. These wee cottages, therefore, provided a constant supply of children to play with and mainly through them, I got to know Blairmains well. Its sights, its sounds and even its smells were a source of wonder to me and, along with the extensive buildings which formed three sides of a square (open to the south), I regarded the whole place as quite magical and looked on John with envy. The next best thing to living on a farm is, I suppose, playing on one and this I started to do pretty regularly.

Behind the northern side of the out-buildings, but joined to them, was an open ended barn in which bales of straw were stored and this, along with the stackyard which it faced, became the centre of our activities – out of the way of the farm's working area but close enough for the occasional adult eye to be cast in our direction.

The bales, a by-product of the previous harvest threshing and used as bedding and feed for the in-wintered bullocks, made wonderful building-blocks and we leapt and tumbled and dived and swung from one straw den to another – a warm, safe, slightly scratchy, boyish bliss. If it was time for John's tea or our bedlam suggested concomitant chaos, Jock would appear, sweep off his bunnet and scratch his head in one smooth, well-practised movement and deliver his immortal injunction – "Away hame y'wee buggers!" So off we 'wee buggers' would trot having already discovered there was no malice in it – that he didn't mean never come back; it was just Jock's way of saying play's-over-for-today-chaps.

On a predominantly arable farm such as Blairmains then was, the labour-intensive season of the year was summer and extra hands were always welcome – even hands as comparatively small and unskilled as mine. I was probably about twelve when, to my huge delight, I first went on the hay pay-roll; I mean, I was already in love with the concept of farmlife so to be invited to do something constructive *and* to be paid for doing it was rather more than I would have dared hope.

Not a great deal of hay is made now; silage is king for the simple reason that at least two crops can be gathered in a season and the fields that once displayed the various stages of hay-making now go straight from lush, grassy growth to black plastic encased rolls of silage looking for all the world like a scatter of giant rabbit droppings. Here and there, though, hay is grown but its winning is a much less complicated business than fifty years ago. It lies in swaths after cutting and when it has dried for two or three days, it's turned to give the underside a similar period of airing and drying; at this point, any similarity between practices of then and now ceases. Today, the hay is simply hoovered up and deposited on to the field like so many big fat wheels which lie around for further drying before being collected and taken back to some storage point on the farm. How different things used to be.

In 1948 when I first played a small part in the process, hay was made by men and horses. Blairmains' two pre-war Fordson tractors had a minor role; these simple pull-'em, push-'em machines had their uses in other tasks about the farm, but they were not major contributors to the winning of the hay. Incidentally, I wonder what a driver of one of those primitive vehicles, stotting about on the spring-leaf supported metal seat and exposed to the whims of a Scottish winter, would make of one of today's monsters with its heated cab, built-in radio/cassette player and a system of hydraulics that could probably thread a needle or take the top off an egg if pressed.

After the cutting and turning, the swaths were tumbled together by the great horse-rake; working across the cut, three or four would be dragged into one and then released from their confinement as a foot-pedal was depressed and the big, curved tines rose clashingly and then dropped to gather more swaths. The next stage involved man and pitchfork. With one of both to each augmented swath, the hay was built up into small heaps called 'quiles' – each probably about three feet high and as wide at the base. This continued until every row had been divided up and the hayfield sported a rash of quiles in neat formation; these were left to air and mature before the next step.

The quiles were now formed into bigger mounds of hay called 'rucks' and this was where a boy was at his most useful; it was his job to tramp down each quile as it was forked on to the 'slipe,' a low-slung, flat cart like a section of flooring on wheels which was pulled from quile to quile by one of the farm horses. Since it moved between rows, hay was being slung at him from both sides, so the tramper had to keep going or he could disappear under a mischievously thrown forkful. After maybe eight quiles had been loaded and tramped, the time came to dump the ruck. With the boy face down and spread-eagled on top and a couple of men steadying the rear with their forks, a lever at the front of the slipe was pulled causing the floor to tip up; at this point, horse and slipe moved forward and the ruck gently slid off the smooth boarding. Occasionally a badly tramped ruck might topple and have to be rebuilt on the ground to the red-cheeked shame of the tramper, but this was rare. After sliding down the steep sided ruck (by this time about eight feet high), the boy had to leap on the already moving slipe to start building the next one; meanwhile, two ropes were crossed at right angles over the recently formed ruck and tied on hay-twists at its foot – this to offer some stability in the face of any frivolous summer winds.

Making hay is a sweaty, dusty business even if the sun isn't shining, so we all needed access to some sort of lubrication. Hanging from a shaft of the slipe and in the shade of the horse's great bulk was a big milk-can filled with water containing several handfuls of oatmeal; a strange combination but a remarkably refreshing drink; mind you, with the drouth we had on us, dish-water might have been just as welcome. The purpose of the oatmeal, I gather, was to help keep the water cool; perhaps it also provided a bit of nourishment for flagging muscles.

Not surprisingly, we were always at the mercy of the weather. Hay tended to be worked anytime from late June onwards and there was a nagging fear in every farmer's mind that, should the weather go against him, the harvest might be on him before his hay was safely won, so, if it wasn't actually raining, we made hay and if the sun shone, we made it for longer.

I think *my* working day began at 8.00am and went on 'til 5.00pm with a modest lunchbreak, but if it was dry and sunny, 'lowsin' time could be extended to 8.00pm or beyond and herein lay one of my simple delights. On a day when, clearly, we would be working late, Mrs Eadie and Elizabeth would appear at 5 o'clock bearing sustenance in the form of a large can of hot, sweet tea and a big basket of mugs and sandwiches – thickly sliced plain bread (no namby-pamby pan loaves for working-men!) filled with pale, creamy butter and rich, raspberry jam – products of milking-parlour and garden. Pitchforks were stuck in the ground, the horse got a twist or two of hay and then, after the ritual removal of bunnets and brow-sweat which revealed jaunty, well defined lines between brown faces and white brows and scalps, we settled down at the foot of a ruck to enjoy this simple and welcome food.

These breaks probably lasted for twenty to twenty-five minutes at most – just enough time to include a pipe, tamped and carefully lit or a slice of 'baccy cut from a thick-black plug and chewed with obvious relish (I tried a bit once – absolutely foul). After conspicuously consulting his pocket-watch, Jock brought the brief idyll to an end by scratching his head, carefully replacing and adjusting his bunnet and getting stiffly to his feet with an enigmatic but significant, "Aye, well..." The boldest of the men might peer pointedly at his own timepiece, but to no effect – we were back at the hay.

The last act of this extended performance was the stacking. The seemingly countless rucks were brought to the stackyard from the far flung corners of the several hayfields to be gobbled up by the voracious jaws of the great hay-hoist; thus did the many become about half a dozen huge stacks, each as big as a house, which completely hid Blairmains from Blairlogie's view.

The hoist, a simple but effective device, consisted of a stout and very long pole placed vertically at the mid-point of the brushwood base of the stack-to-be. (This kept the precious hay clear of the wet ground and thus prolonged its goodness over the winter to come.) Wedges at the bottom and guys from the top kept it upright. A lesser pole was slung horizontally across this in such a way that it could twist freely and be raised or lowered as necessary. Attached, by means of a rope and pulleys to one end of the horizontal was the hay-fork. Hinged in the middle and spring-cocked to allow it to be folded in to a load of hay and then opened to release the load, this was a metal rectangle of, perhaps, four feet by two with a slightly curved tine at each corner; the release mechanism on the hinged, central cross-piece was controlled by a rope threaded through pulleys and eyelets to the other end of the horizontal and, thence, down to the hand of the director of operations – Jock.

Building a haystack was men's work – two of them tramping each load of hay after swinging it to the required spot with their forks and holding it there 'til Jock tugged the release rope and then ducking and weaving away from the hay-fork's big tines as it swung erratically before heading for the ground and the next load. And then there was the height at which they worked, especially in the latter stages. No, definitely not for boys; besides, I was well pleased with my particular job.

The other end of the hay-fork rope was attached to a swingletree which, in turn, was attached to a horse's harness. As the horse moved forward, hay-fork and load went up; when the horse hit reverse, the by now empty hay-fork came down. Simple, but the horse had to have a minder – often that was me.

Until the Second World War, the Clydesdale was the draught horse of Scotland and the standing of a farm was measured in the number of pairs it worked. (A pair of Clydes was the power unit for many tasks.) With no certainty at all, I think I recollect Blairmains' stable having six stalls thus suggesting that, in earlier times, it had been a three pair establishment. Now, in the late 1940s, with two tractors already in their shed and further mechanisation soon to appear, only two of the stalls were occupied – by Tam, a temperamental gelding , and Rosie, a mare whose nature reflected her name. Tam, with a confusion of stunted hormones and emotions coursing through his huge frame was a man's beast; in fact he had two pet hates – **i**) walking backwards and **ii**) small boys who attempted to make him do just that. On such an occasion, the neck would arch and the head twist as he endeavoured to get the source of his irritation into view and then one could find oneself being minutely examined by a malevolent and increasingly white eye. That was the signal for a small person to retreat – and rapidly. Rosie, with beautiful, long-lashed, dark eyes had no objections to **i**) and **ii**) above and, if treated with consideration, was sweetness itself. So, Rosie and I formed an unlikely partnership, me walking backwards as she advanced and then vice versa. The minder *had* to keep watching the action; if Rosie was started or stopped too soon, a volley of mixed language from Jock, the trampers, the hay-fork loaders and anyone else in the vicinity would assail his ears and add much colour to them.

The walls of a well built stack had to slope outwards ever so slightly – this to encourage rain-water to drain off more easily. In other words, each layer of hay overhung the previous one by a wee bit. When the stack was, possibly, twenty feet high (and I must own to guessing dimensions here) each layer became considerably narrower than the previous one; in this way, a pitched roof of hay was formed, again to encourage the shedding of rain-water. After hand raking all round to present a smooth surface to the elements, the trampers hurled forks and rakes to an appropriately hay-cushioned area below and then grasping the hay-fork, they floated slowly groundward. A network of ropes previously slung across the new stack and tied to many bricks, helped to anchor the hay against autumnal gales. The hoist was dismantled and set up by the brushwood base of the next stack-to-be and the whole exercise was repeated until all the hay was gathered in.

I think I worked in the Blairmains hayfields for four seasons. (I was in Canada for the whole of what would have been my fifth which provided a natural break and I never went back – anyway, I was getting too big for ruck-tramping.) Of course there were moments of monotony and times when I'd rather have been doing something else, but the overall experience was good and the memories are happy.

Blairlogie Thistle

By stretching the imagination close to breaking point, I like to think there's a tenuous link between a misplaced German landmine and our football team.

On Saturday, 20th July, 1940, an enemy bomber – and here there are two theories: **a)** it was being chased from the Glasgow area or **b)** it was there specifically to strike at the big REME depot at Forthside (take your pick) – released its landmines imperfectly over Stirling. One fell harmlessly on a field, but the other fell harmfully on the ground of King's Park FC at Forthbank.

It's interesting to read contemporary accounts of the incident. In order to deny the enemy information about the success or failure of such missions, reporting restrictions forbade the use of place-names; thus the Stirling Journal referred to the raid as...

'Moonlight Attack on South-East Town'

Having rid the plane of its burden, the crew then flew low over the town with guns blazing – this, no doubt, to encourage the good citizens to keep their good heads down. They did. Anyway, the outcome of the attack was that the REME depot remained intact but Stirling's football supporters were denied their Saturday afternoon pleasure for the rest of the war.

In 1946, a former director of King's Park FC – local coal-merchant 'Tam' Fergusson – brought league football back to the town when he created Stirling Albion FC. (I believe the Albion bit came from the fact that several of his lorries were of that make.) This enterprise was greeted with a fervent enthusiasm out of all proportion to its position within the Scottish League structure; as 'new boys', the Albion had to start at the bottom of the pile which, in those days, meant Division 'C'. A pitch had been carved out of the capacious grounds of Annfield House – a handsome 18th century mansion which, to my conservationist father's horror, was destined to contain the club's changing-rooms, offices and the like; used and abused by most; appreciated by few. To begin with, spectators stood round the playing area while those wishing to be above it all were obliged to balance, somewhat precariously, on one of Fergusson's coal lorries which were dotted around the pitch. When the lorries had gone and terracing and proper stands were in place, Davie's father used to take us along to many of the home matches – and that's how it all started.

Filled with images of our heroes – Jock Whiteford (dominating), Geordie Henderson (dashing), Geordie 'feet' Dick (dazzling) – as they did metaphorical battle with the likes of Leith Athletic, Edinburgh City or Montrose, it was natural that the first thing we wanted to do on getting home was to start belting a ball about. We'd rush along to the field in front of Dougie and Mossie's house and, meeting up with others of a like mind, run around frantically giving wretched impressions of action from the match.

Ever since there's been a ball to be kicked and a goal to be scored, boys have cast their jackets on the ground for goal-posts – and we were no different. Though reasonably adequate, they could be the cause of warm debate...

"GOAL!!!"

"Naw it wuznae – 's a post."

"Wuz not!"

"Wuz sot!"

...and so on. Usually, the owner of the ball acted as ultimate arbiter and, clearly, his decision was coloured by which side he played for. The threat to remove the ball quelled any further dispute. We got round this area of contention by 'borrowing' four fence stobs which, at a stroke, halved the potential for argument; *height* of the shot was now the only debatable dimension.

The field has long since disappeared under a car-park and its attendant wilderness to the east of the village but, in its day, the turf was good and, once we'd got rid of the thistles (hence our name), we had a serviceable, if small and slightly misshapen, football pitch. This became the centre of our end-of-school day, weekend and holiday activities. With no distractions in the shape of TV, computer games or the like, we were out playing as often as parents, weather, daylight, 'Dick Barton – Special Agent' and the Saturday evening football results would allow.

The north side of the pitch was part bordered by scrub and small trees and part by a chicken-wire fence which divided pitch from the small garden in front of Dougie and Mossie's house. Considering our far from perfect ball-control, it's surprising that the windows facing the pitch remained as relatively unscathed as they did. Early on there may have been a broken pane or two, but the threat of expulsion from our footballing arena certainly encouraged caution when propelling the ball in that particular direction. The south side was bordered by the main road with a stone dyke in between. Since we were a couple of feet below road-level, the dyke was higher on our side which led to a local adaptation of the laws of the game; playing a quick 'one-two' with the wall became an accepted method of beating an opponent. Of course, this depended on the player of the one-two having the skill to place the ball exactly where he wanted it in order to collect the rebound. Should the manoeuvre be less than carefully executed, it could become a one-oops! as the ball sailed over the wall and a one-oops!-BANG! if it was unlucky enough to land under a passing vehicle. That would be the end of a modern ball but, in those days, durability was stitched into every panel.

Footballs used to be built to last *and* to be repaired. The leather panelled outer-case had a lace-up opening which allowed an inflatable bladder to be inserted or removed as necessary. This was blown up by means of an integral tube –

perhaps two inches long – into which an inflator, screwed to the end of a bicycle pump, was pushed. This cunning device contained a ball-bearing which allowed air in when the pump was discharging, but stopped it getting out when the pump was recharging. If the ball had been subjected to a one-oops!-BANG!, the damage could be severe enough to warrant a replacement panel or two; this was a job for a cobbler. If the bladder was repairable, we did it – if not, a new one was needed but it was the *next* stage that could prove troublesome. Once the bladder had been inflated inside the case, the integral tube had to be doubled over and tied to prevent air escaping; it then had to be pushed inside and the lace-up opening pulled tight and flat. This was the problem and, more often than not, we were left with an ungainly swelling which could induce a similarly ungainly swelling on a young brow if the two came into contact.

If I take an arbitrary age of, say, fourteen-and-under and then compare a village child count of today with that of fifty years ago, the figures are interesting; the Blairlogie of 1998 has about eight in that category whereas, half a century ago, there appears to have been twenty five or thereabouts. Of this number, about half would have been girls and, of the remainder, another half would have been too wee – more likely to *fall* over a comparatively heavy ball than kick it. They were a nuisance and actively discouraged – unless, of course, such a one happened to own a ball and we, at the time, happened to require access to one. That was a very different story and oh, how we would fawn over the wee pain...

"Great shot, Wullie" (or some such name) as the shilpit cratur stubbed his toe on the ball propelling it all of three feet...

"Run onto this pass, Wullie. YES!" as the pins were knocked from under him leading to a very close examination of the turf. As our competitive interest in proceedings intensified, wee Wullie would receive less and less attention; soon he would be ignored completely. This was a dangerous time. Should his girns and tears not be immediately and appropriately soothed, progress in the compelling Blairlogie v. Rest of the World thriller could be brought to an abrupt halt by the angry voice of a wee Wullie parent...

"Heh, youse yins! Gie the bairn his ba' or else..."

'Or else' never sounded an attractive alternative so, with poor grace, wee Wullie would get his ball and, as like as not, we would get the full extent of his tongue for our trouble. But I digress. Back to the demographics of childhood. This left roughly half a dozen to pursue a ball relentlessly and, eventually, to form the nucleus of Blairlogie Thistle.

Round about this time, Davie joined the Menstrie Scouts and was pleasantly surprised to discover that not every young Menstrie heart was hardened against the youth of Blairlogie – that not every lad from that village intuitively had it in for us; friendships were formed and communications established. Rennie McOwan was probably the first from Menstrie to come along and join us in our, more or less, daily kick-and-rush and, I should imagine, he and Davie were instrumental in arranging the first of *very* many Blairlogie v. Menstrie matches. Of course, there was still the small problem of numbers. Menstrie, with no boypower shortages, was quite happy to accommodate us – if we only had seven (including Rennie) then *they'd* just use seven; if, on the other hand, we'd care to 'borrow' some players – not the best ones of course – both sides could be at full strength and this is what we did. Eventually, Blairlogie would 'adopt' three or four players from Menstrie who, quite happy to join us, would become full members of our team. Blairlogie Thistle FC was nearly up and running and kicking.

The organisational abilities shown in the 'Gang' days were now brought to bear on our new venture; close to having the numbers to *make* a team, we wanted to *look* like a team. We needed a strip.

Blairlogie today is, overwhelmingly, a middle-class community: fifty years ago, things were very different. The few middle-class households were, probably, reasonably comfortably off, but this was not the case within quite a number of the working-class majority – there wasn't money to spare for the gratification of an apparent whim... "You want a football strip? Save for it!"...was the understandable parental attitude. Now, all of us got pocket-money in one form or another – either for jobs done or (whisper it) as a gratuity – so, in a splendid spirit of co-operation, we elected to stick together and save up for a set of strips. A sum of 3d. per team-member per week was agreed and I, as secretary/treasurer, collected and held the money. My mother, more sensitive to the potential pitfalls ahead than her enthusiastic son, insisted on auditing my accounts-book frequently.

We were very determined and disciplined – if a member missed a week's payment then he owed double the following week and, in this way, we reached our goal remarkably quickly. According to my accounts-book (yes, it's in front of me now) our first contribution to the fund was on 1st Oct., 1949 and by 26th Nov., 1949, we'd raised enough to buy some strips. Before anyone with a jot of numeracy starts trying to make sense of this, let me make a couple of points. A football strip in those days cost about 10/6d. *and* our income did not depend entirely on weekly subs; dotted around the book are quite a lot of entries, simply designated 'Gift', ranging from 3d. to 2/9d. (over a quarter of a strip!) – these tended to come from adults keen to support our enterprise. Two weeks prior to our purchase, we appear to have held a Sale – selling what and to whom, goodness knows – which raised the sum of 27/9d. (two and a half strips). Oh, and I see an entry after the one giving details of the strips transaction – 'We owe Mrs Kelsall 13/8d.'...and then... 'PAID'.

At the time of all this high finance, my mother and I were staying in Glasgow during the week and coming home at weekends – she was working with the BBC Scottish Variety Orchestra (featured soloist) and I was in my first term at Kelvinside Academy (mediocre scholar). Adult advice suggested that Glasgow would offer a wider choice and better deals than Stirling, so the task of buying the strips was entrusted to me and, one Sunday evening in late November, I returned to that city clutching the entire wealth of Blairlogie

Thistle FC. At some point during the following week, mother and I did a bit of shopping around and, finally, a deal was struck in the Sports Department of Arnott-Simpson's in Argyle Street; in return for £3.11.2d (including the maternal 13/8d), I proudly took posession of a parcel of seven matching football strips.

Price had always been our yardstick and, therefore, I wasn't too concerned about colour – my team-mates were. The looks and expressions of disbelief when I opened the parcel to reveal seven bright yellow strips ranged from a mild... "Ah'm no' wearin' *thon*"...to considerably stronger. My protests to the effect that they'd only cost 10/2d each fell on less than interested ears; in short, I was far from flavour of the month. After further caustic comment on their part and a huffy silence on mine, it was at least agreed that we should have a dress-rehearsal. This took place the following day and, when worn with white shorts, it was reluctantly conceded that the strips didn't look too bad. The acid test was yet to come though.

The next weekend an eight-a-side had been arranged with Menstrie (this was just prior to the 'adoption' previously mentioned) – the first public airing of our new strip. Our opponents turned up in their usual motley collection of shirts and jerseys with an isolated strip or two and then we revealed our yellow and white glory. *Well...* the yells, catcalls and whistles that greeted this golden vision was almost unnerving; two or three on our side – those who'd objected most vehemently to my innocent choice – reacted angrily... "It wuz nuthin' t'dae wi' me – it's his fau't."...pointing accusatory fingers in my direction. I've no idea of the score but, in the general rough-and-tumble of such a contest, at least our players were easily and quickly identifiable. Ever after, we were known as 'The Canaries' and that was an end to the ribbing; indeed, on 5th Jan., 1950, I bought three more because by that time we were up to full strength. (We already had a goalie's jersey. Two actually.)

Towards the end of 1950, things changed. We were, by now, bigger and stronger and I think Dougie and Mossie's parents were increasingly concerned for the safety of their property; a few little boys chasing after a ball was one thing – a lot of bigger boys kicking lumps out of each other in an atmosphere of inter-village rivalry was another. We were given notice to quit our wee pitch so, inevitably, all Blairlogie Thistle's future matches were to be of the 'Away' variety. Then some of the village grown-ups stepped in. With the help of R. M. Bruce of the Stirling Observer, a footballing symposium was arranged for the evening of 4th December and held in the Reading Room. The Observer of 7.12.50 reported the event at some length (18 column inches!); the following is a top-and-tail version...

SOCCER BRAINS TRUST
MONDAY'S BLAIRLOGIE SESSION
FOOTBALL STARS' ADVICE

The lads of the recently-formed Blairlogie village football team – Blairlogie Thistle – sat enthralled on Monday night as they absorbed the words of soccer wisdom that came across to them from the platform of their Village Hall.

As well they might; for there was about sixty years' professional football-playing experience behind the soccer "brains trust" speaking to them from the platform. That joint length of service could be claimed by Duncan Ogilvie, former Motherwell and Scotland winger; Bob Shankly, ex-Falkirk and Scotland player, now the Falkirk club manager, and Archie Gourlay, of Stirling, who kept goal for the Scottish senior clubs, Hibs and Partick Thistle...

...Mr Moultrie R. Kelsall, well-known BBC broadcaster, compered in racy fashion during the evening. He said the lads had started the club in Blairlogie and the adults there thought, as they had done something for themselves, the grown-ups should do something for them. Mr John Eadie of Blairmains had given them the field to play on, Mr D. McLeish had given them goal-posts and Mr R. M. Bruce, "Stirling Observer" had arranged for the sporting personalities to come along that evening. Accordionists Grace Barr and Marie Roy played at an interlude.

The football quiz winner was Alec Wilson, Loaning Bank, Menstrie who won the special prize gifted by Palmers Ltd., sports outfitters, Stirling. Second prize was won by Maurice Evans, The Orchard, Blairlogie.

Blairlogie Thistle aka 'The Canaries'
Back (l. to r.): Kelsall; Evans, D.; Muirhead; Evans, M.; Stephens, G.
Front (l. to r.): Wilson; Stark; Smith; Eadie; McLeish; Stephens, B.; Lindsay.

Blairlogie Thistle v. Naemoor School (Mrs Janet Grieve's successor to Riverview).
Waiting to catch a bus to Rumbling Bridge, 25.2.1950.
Back (l. to r.): Evans, M.; McPherson; McOwan; Muirhead; Evans, D.
Front (l. to r.): Bryce; McLeish; Stephens; Eadie.
Photographer: Kelsall

Votes of thanks to the "brains trust" and the artistes were given by Mr Kelsall, who was thanked by Mr Duncan Muirhead, and Mr D. McLeish thanked Mr R. M. Bruce for organising the entertainment.

Naturally, all this adult attention was very gratifying – I even bought a hardback notebook in which to record this new chapter in the history of Blairlogie Thistle FC. But something was wrong.

Our new pitch was a long way from the village. A field opposite Witches' Craig caravan park, it was huge, a bit rough and, I suppose, impersonal. If you went *there* looking for someone to kick-around with, it was likely to be a futile search.

Despite an optimistic preface...

Blairlogie Thistle FC.
The goal-posts, gifted by Mr McLeish, were put up on the night of Sunday 4th March **[1951]**, and the marking of Hydro Park **[our name]**, lent to us by Mr Eadie, was completed on Saturday 10th March.

... my notebook contains precious little else – four and a half pages of 'reports' on seven widely scattered matches (only two of which were played on our new pitch with its new goal-posts). All our footballing activity seems to have ended on Wednesday, 2nd Jan., 1952 with a game against the auld enemy – Menstrie.

Venue: Menstrie.
Blairlogie Thistle: Eadie; D. Evans, M. Evans; McLeish, Brownlee; Kelsall, Curly, Smith, B. Stephens, G. Stephens.

Menstrie: ?
Score: Blairlogie 9 Menstrie 3 (Half-time: 5 – 1)

Scorers for Blairlogie: Brownlee (2), Smith (2), M. Evans (2pens), G. Stephens, Curly, Kelsall.

Ah well, at least we went out on a high note and I even scored a goal. There weren't too many of *them* over the years.

Footnote: Three, who turned out for Blairlogie Thistle on several occasions, went on to slightly higher things. Jack Hinchliff played for Aston Villa, Laurie Thomson for Partick Thistle and his brother, Robert 'Tiger' Thomson, for Liverpool.

Uncle Arthur

As a child, all adults known to me were addressed as Mr or Mrs unless they were close family friends; in this case, even though they were kith rather than kin, their Christian names received the prefix Uncle or Aunt. In this way, Mr and Mrs Black from Aberdeen became my Uncle Arthur and Auntie Win.

She, though a kindly and friendly soul, did not share a thirteen-year-old boy's interests; Auntie Win, therefore, sticks in my memory for three reasons only, one of which was a consequence of the other two. Completely hooked on crossword puzzles and cigarettes, she never attempted one of the former without one of the latter stuck (often literally) between her lips; the column of smoke which drifted up the front of her face left her predominantly white hair sporting a permanent yellowy-brown quiff.

Arthur Black was part of the coterie of talented professional or semi-professional actors and writers my father gathered round him in the Aberdeen broadcasting days of the 1930s. A teacher of craft subjects in a secondary-modern school, Uncle Arthur spent much of his spare time writing and taking part in sketches for various radio programmes – especially the children's favourite, 'Aberdeen Animals'. A stocky man of medium height with an easy smile and trim moustache, his rimlessly bespectacled eyes sparkled from under the bushiest eyebrows I had ever seen; they quite took the attention away from a bald pate fringed by short, white hair – well, almost. Arthur delighted in his Doric heritage and his conversation was always peppered with 'fit like's, 'fa's 'at's, 'loons', 'quines' an' a' sorts.

Keen on football and cricket, he and I got on splendidly despite an age gap of fifty-plus years. The one problem in our relationship, from my point of view, was Uncle Arthur's car or, rather, the way he drove it.

A 1936 Hillman Minx, it had, as I remember, three forward gears and an unusual speedometer. This was no ordinary dial and needle calibrated to suggest speeds far outwith the vehicle's capability; rather it was, I imagine, a rotating disc placed behind the dashboard and the relative speed of the car at any given time was viewed through a little opening or window. To this day, I've no idea of that particular model's alleged top speed; certainly, in Uncle Arthur's canny hands, there was never the slightest possibility of finding out. Bear in mind the time of which I write was, perhaps, three or four years after the war when roads were blissfully uncluttered things – this was a mercy.

A story, probably apocryphal, circulated of Uncle Arthur, in a fit of rage or exuberance, once causing the rotating disc to display the magic 20 mph mark – Auntie Win shrieking and hanging on for dear life at his side; top speed whenever I sat beside him was 15. I used to gaze at that speedometer with fascinated disbelief because, even though our family was car-less at the time, I had enough experience of different vehicles and their drivers to realise that Uncle Arthur was quite unlike other road users – horse drawn stuff apart. Still, so long as this little quirk stayed within the family, as it were, I could live with it. Unfortunately it didn't.

In summer, at which season the Blacks were wont to appear for part of their annual holiday, Blairlogie Thistle FC (football) became Blairlogie CC (cricket). The same boypower shortage applied as did the method by which it was overcome. A match due to be played against a team from Alloa at that town's magnificent Paton and Baldwin sports ground (now, tragically, a housing estate) coincided with the yearly visit. Under normal circumstances, the Blairlogie contingent would cycle the four-or-so miles to the venue, but, for various

Win and Arthur Black in their Aberdeen garden.

Our cat ignoring Arthur's car. The four cyclists would have had this view of it before getting their legs going.

reasons, three bikes were out of action.

"Dinna fash!" quoth Uncle Arthur, following this with the suggestion that he would drive me, the bike-less boys and our 'bitties o' bats an' things' to the match *and* he would stand as our umpire. I couldn't refuse and my heart sank.

Departure time arrived and my worst fears were soon to be realised. Three respectful team-members sat in the back with assorted equipment while I hunched glumly in the front, eyes downcast. Behind us, four cyclists waited for the off hoping, as was the slightly risky way, to catch the slipstream of the car and thus save a bit of leg-work; little did they know.

We moved smoothly away and at 5mph, first-gear was abandoned for second; this took us up to 10 at which point the change to top was effortlessly made; as I feared, the disc ceased its steady movement at 15 and I groaned – but quietly.

Restlessness, whispering and movement, as the back-seat passengers twisted to look out of the rear windscreen, was followed by a shout of laughter at some antic of one of the cyclists. I stared furiously at the little window willing the disc to surge to ever higher numbers and thus silence the giggles and sniggers; it didn't and Uncle Arthur was oblivious to it all. My shame was complete when, one by one, the four cyclists overtook us and hurtled, comparatively speaking, into the distance and out of sight.

"Impatient loons!" was the driver's only comment.

I sat hunched of shoulder, wretched of expression and watched the scenery trickle past.

And the match? Thanks to some less than impartial decisions by our umpire, we actually won which raised Uncle Arthur's standing in the eyes of the rest of the team if not the opposition. And my own contribution? I'd love to report that my plucky, match-winning innings came to an untimely end when my flashing square-cut unluckily top-edged to second slip off a brute of a fast, rising, off-cutter. In reality, so preoccupied was I with the prospect of the return journey that I totally missed the innocuous, looping full-toss that gently – almost apologetically – fell on my stumps; nor did my duck do much for our total.

Our Car

In 1924, Noel Macklin built a car in his garage at Cobham, Surrey. It was the first of a modest line of vehicles marketed under the slightly optimistic name Invicta and though there was no denying the quality, the low production meant that it would never mount a serious challenge to the big boys. Nevertheless, Invictas found favour with many well-known drivers of the day – people like Donald Healey and Raymond Mays; the latter, in his 4.5-litre low-chassis model, broke the sports car hill-climb record at Shelsley Walsh leaving a Tourist Trophy Mercedes-Benz SSKL trailing in his dust. One who did much to promote the qualities of the car was a lady called Violet Cordery who, belying her Christian name, undertook some daunting endurance tests. In 1926, at the famous Brooklands racing circuit, she covered 5000 miles at an average speed of 73mph but, a few years later, that feat was dwarfed when, with her sister, she drove 70,000 miles in the same number of minutes. It was said that only someone else's sanity prevailed to dissuade her from her ultimate demonstration of the Invicta's reliability – driving up the Great North Road from London to Edinburgh in reverse!

So, what's with this rigmarole of an introduction? Well, in 1938 my father bought one; already seven years old, she cost him £40, but he was well pleased and Vicky (so called after the Kelsall penchant for nicknaming the inanimate) became part of our small family. At age two, everything seemed huge to me especially this 30hp, 4.5-litre, two ton monster and I have one hazy memory of being in the back with Mary (my nanny) while way in front of me were my parents and stretching even further into the distance was the shiny radiator-cap and headlights. I think we must have had a puncture, because I can remember bricks being called for – presumably to help the jack support Vicky's weight – and then Mary taking me for a walk possibly out of earshot of father's increasingly exasperated commentary.

Come the war and almost immediate fuel rationing, Vicky became a liability. Even when going like a sewing machine, her great engine only produced 15 miles to the gallon – and although Broadcasting was a reserved occupation it offered no scope for a car-user allowance of petrol coupons; she was trapped. A family friend who lived in rural Essex persuaded a local farmer to allow Vicky the use of a shed which stood some slight distance from the friend's house; this on the understanding that just as soon as sufficient coupons had been collected, Vicky would be heading for Scotland. I regret to say that sufficient coupons were *not* collected, and Vicky sat out the war and more in this less than solid wooden shed.

I think the call came in 1947 – whether before or after father left the BBC I'm not sure. The Essex friend had been told by the farmer that he'd chased two men who appeared to be attempting to tow Vicky out of her fairly isolated shed with the aid of a lorry. According to the farmer, these Essex wide-boys (or others of a similarly broad inclination) had already paid her a visit and removed that which was readily removable. This piece of intelligence concentrated the paternal mind wonderfully.

Until August, 1947, there was a basic petrol ration which allowed the private motorist enough fuel to do 270 miles per month. The suddenness of the news from Essex didn't give him much time, but, one way or another, he obtained a sufficiency of petrol coupons (he hoped) and having enlisted the professional expertise of a pal, David Mowat, who ran the transport-pool at the BBC's Glasgow studios, they headed south to the rescue. An unhappy sight was waiting for them. The shed was in a state of collapse – indeed, had it not been

Father (left) and David Mowat hiding the worst of Vicky's wartime neglect. The retreat from Essex, c. 1947.

Vicky, having been sold, about to return to Essex, 1983.

for the support offered by Vicky's considerable bulk, the structure would have fallen down long before. The Essex wide-boys had smashed the front, nearside window in order to get inside and, now, contented hens perched on, under and in the car. The shed's earthen floor, having given up the unequal struggle to support two tons of Invicta, now snugly embraced all four wheels not far short of axle level. To the annoyance of the hens, a closer inspection revealed that Vicky's previous visitors had pinched both spare wheels, all the hide-leather seat cushions, bits and pieces like the windscreen wipers and motor, the radiator cap and, most destructively of all, they'd used a hack-saw on the dashboard to remove the clock and the petrol guage.

Maybe the forgiving nature of the floor had something to do with it, but, by a miracle, the tyre walls were not ruined and all retained the air that Mr Mowat and father laboriously pumped into them. Mercifully, radiator and block had been drained in 1939 so there were no cracks, but the pistons – all six of them – were quite lovingly attached to their respective cylinder-walls. Lights and the coil ignition were non-functioning due to the depredations of mice over the years; fortunately, the Meadows engine which powered Vicky was a dual-ignition job, so she was able to run on the magneto.

David Mowat worked wonders and, aided by his pretty unskilled labourer, the engine was running within a day – hirpling, perhaps, rather than running; one of the twin SU carburettors was less than happy and remained so throughout the journey north. So, with a small log jammed in the top of the radiator, straw-filled sacks for driver and passenger to sit on and oil, grease and petrol in, more or less, the right places, Vicky's considerable nose was pointed in the direction of Scotland; her long and undignified incarceration was at an end.

Her existence, thereafter, could best be described as nomadic. She wandered from specialist to specialist and city to city as her years of neglect and abuse were put right. Petrol, already scarce, was shortly to become scarcer and that, coupled with all the other shortages of the time, meant father wasn't in a position to do much with her even had he wanted to, so each stopping-off place became her temporary home. Extraordinary though it may seem, I would think it was a couple of years before she finally came to live with us in Blairlogie; even then, since her garage had not yet been built and since father was not prepared to let all that protracted and expensive refurbishment sit around outside, space was rented for her in a commercial garage in Menstrie.

Vicky was, I suppose, a variation on my father's conservationist theme – she needed restoring and that's all there was to it. He had never looked on her as anything other than an occasional and alternative form of transport – alternative to the public variety which he regarded as perfectly adequate and certainly as cheap. So, in a way, Vicky was almost destined to become mine; mother *couldn't* drive, father as often as not *wouldn't* drive which left the way open to me once I learned the skill. Not as straightforward as it sounds.

Confronted by a fraction of today's volume of traffic, the L-driver of forty five years ago had it relatively easy. Not so those learning on Invictas. From the instructor's point of view, the chief drawback was the positioning of gear-stick and hand-brake; both of these were on the right of the driver and, therefore, out of reach of the instructor should an emergency arise. He could only hope that his yell of warning/dismay/terror would be enough to bring his pupil back to the real world. From the pupil's point of view, the chief drawback was the lack of synchromesh in the gear-box. Today, a driver depresses clutch, moves gear-stick and releases clutch. Easy! In Vicky this would **a)** make a noise like a heavy machine-gun or **b)** endanger the public as the exploding gear-box sprayed cogs about. The non-synchromesh box requires the driver to depress the clutch, move the stick to neutral, release clutch, dab the accelerator (to synchronise gear-wheel speeds), depress clutch, move stick and, finally, release the clutch again. Sounds complicated? Try doing it as a complete beginner.

Never having had to sit a driving-test – in his day, one just got a licence, a bit of advice on the vehicle one was going to drive and that was it – father was fine for teaching me how to handle Vicky, but he didn't presume to instruct me on the mysteries of the Highway Code; these were for *me* to discover.

My test I remember very clearly. After accompanying me to the centre, father made himself scarce while I went in search of the examiner. Vicky's impressive dimensions induced a sharp intake of breath and a slight hesitancy in a formerly confident step, but the man recovered quickly and we were soon on our way. Not only was my double-declutching noisier than I would have wished, but I singularly failed to follow some of his required changes of direction and I think my three-point developed into, at least, a four-point turn. Then came the Highway Code questions...

"Now then, Mr Kelsall, give me an example of a situation in which it would be inappropriate to accelerate."

I looked at him in disbelief – it was so blindingly obvious. Was it a trick? No. Go for it Robin!

"When you're going to stop."

To this day, I can see the heavenward roll of his eyes as he turned to look out of the nearside window. I can't remember the other questions, but I'll never forget that one.

Was it because I got him back in one piece? Was it because, despite everything, I could obviously handle this leviathan of the road? Was it because I made him laugh? Whatever it was, I passed.

This has now exceeded the boundaries of a 'Blairlogie Boyhood' and I should stop. Just one anecdote before I do; it concerns Vicky and Ben.

He was our Scottish Deerhound – as big in the world of dogs as was Vicky in the world of cars. I never saw Ben in pursuit of a deer but, on the flat, broad acres of Blairmains farm, he was forever putting up hares – not that they were in any danger. He could outrun them with no difficulty but, as soon as he drew near, the hare jinked and was away on a new tack. Ben, with the turning-circle of a single-decker bus, would attempt to adjust to the new direction in a flail of legs and tail and have to start all over again. Great fun for all except, I

Ben in louping mode.

suppose, the hare but, as it always got away, no harm was done.

When we travelled *en famille*, I usually drove with father as co-pilot while my poor mother occupied the rear seat with Ben – she tucked into a small corner while he, sprawled on his big dunlopillo mattress (supported by suitcases twixt rear and front seats), filled the rest. On such occasions, ventilation was essential due to Ben's tendency to let loose anal emissions of great potency; my mother, being closest, bore the brunt of these eruptions. Whenever we stopped – even at traffic-lights – Ben, assuming he could now get out, would stand up thus appearing to fill the rear of the car.

In 1959, I was called up to do my National Service most of which was spent in the Royal Artillery (Plymouth) Band in Oswestry, a small town on the English/Welsh border. It was there I met my wife-to-be; she was a student nurse in the Robert Jones and Agnes Hunt Orthopaedic Hospital about half a mile down the road from our camp. On one occasion, my parents drove down to see us – mother, by this time promoted to co-pilot, sitting in front and Ben occupying the whole of the rear. Having learned that Brenda (w-t-b) would be off-duty and probably in the Nurses' Home, they drove to that block where they were met at the door by a small Welsh maid. While they were asking to see Nurse Gilbert (maiden name of w-t-b), they were aware that small Welsh maid's ever widening eyes were focused on Vicky and Ben – since the car had stopped, he was, of course, standing up. Small Welsh maid ran off to seek Nurse Gilbert in a state of some excitement and, on finding her, blurted...

"Oh, Miss Gilbert, *Miss Gilbert* – people to see you. They're in a charabanc with a donkey in the back!"

Footnote: Two years after my father's death, mother decided she wanted the garage space that Vicky was occupying. *I* certainly couldn't afford to keep or run her so, with a lot of sadness, she was sold. And where was her new home to be? Somewhere in Essex!

Gone Forever

This is about two rows of cottages, a steading and a smallholding that featured large in our childhood; as with the latter, they disappeared a long time ago.

1) Victoria Place

The neighbour failed to get any response to her chapping and, unusually at this time of the morning, the door of the wee cottage was locked. Anxiously, she fetched her husband who forced it with no great difficulty. Nennie Binnie was in her favourite chair by the fireside and, from her position, the neighbours judged that she had died in the act of tying her left boot; the right one was securely laced.

She was christened Janet but, as with many others so named in Scotland, this soon became Jennie and Nennie could well have been her own early attempt to pronounce this. Whatever the derivation, it remained her lifelong name on all but the most formal occasion.

Longevity was, clearly, a characteristic common to both sides of Nennie's family; she was in her 83rd year when she died on that morning of Thursday, 4th July, 1940 while her father, Thomas Binnie (d. 1913), had lived to be ninety-six and her mother, Margaret (d. 1906), was eighty-six at her death. The latter, incidentally, was the daughter of the formidable Peggy Dawson who ran Blairlogie's first post office when it opened in the westernmost of the farm cottages. Dawsons were a long established family in the village so, on her mother's

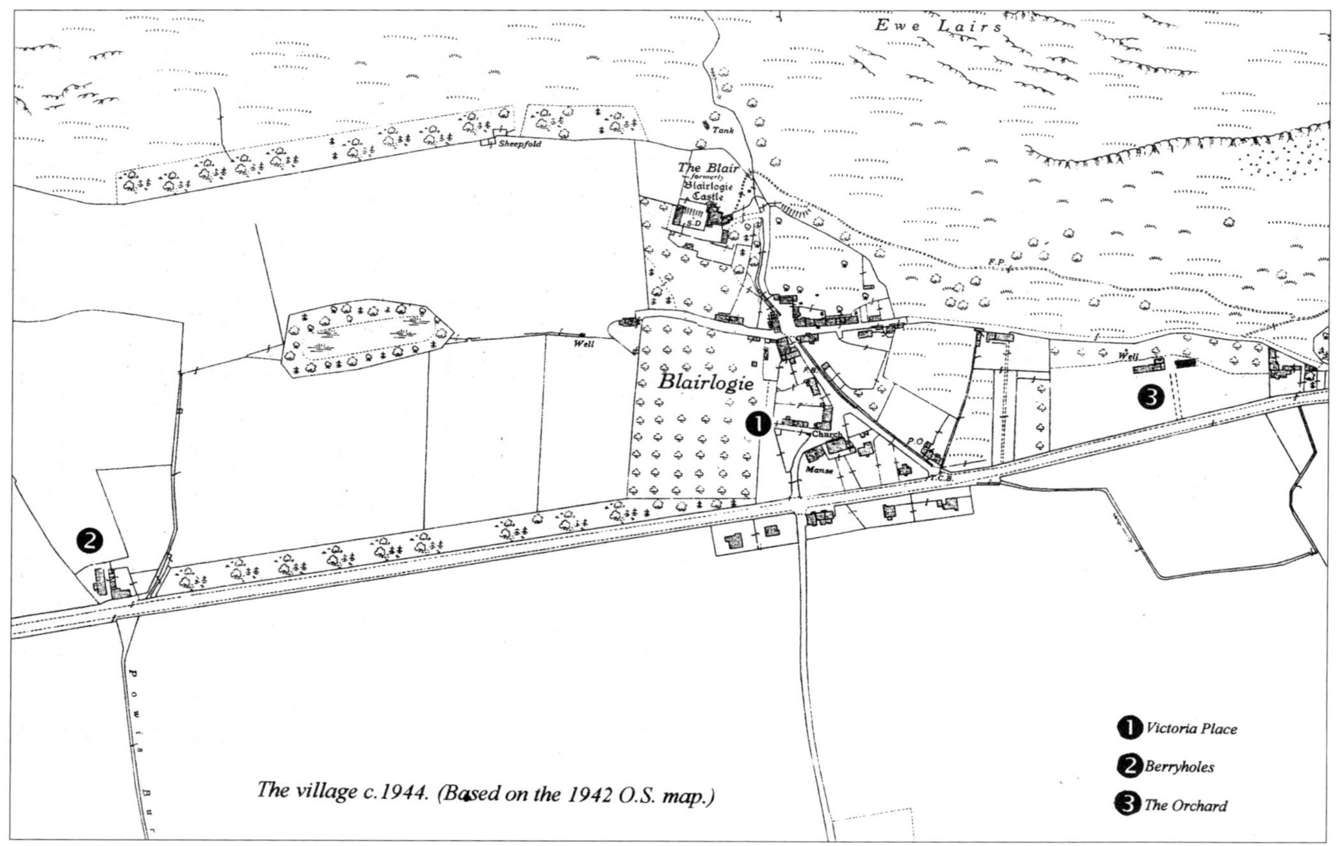

The village c.1944. (Based on the 1942 O.S. map.)

side, Nennie's death ended a continuous Blairlogie connection spanning anything up to 150 years – probably more. It also temporarily ended the habitation of Victoria Place. How a wee row of mid-18th century country cottages came to inherit such a grand, urban name is a mystery. I'm sure it was only ever used by the Post Office and the Local Authority – if at all.

Originally four in number, ours (Kirklea Cottage) was probably the last to be built; certainly it was the most substantial and the only one of two storeys. The others were of mud-mortared rubble with a thatched roof; when the latter became less than watertight, the absentee owner had it covered with corrugated-iron sheeting – a cheap and nasty solution that detracted greatly from the cottages' otherwise picturesque appearance. Photographs going back to the turn of the century show that something had happened to the one abutting upon Kirklea; the front wall is there but the roof isn't. The resultant gap (a blessing as it would turn out) was now a yard – entered by the former front door – in which were two earth-closets and a large coal shed. I imagine this partial demolition was deliberate in order to provide the inhabitants of Victoria Place with these simple amenities; a late-20th century mind can only boggle at what went on before such improvements. So that's how things stood when father first saw Kirklea Cottage not many months after Nennie Binnie's death.

Once empty, such primitive housing was automatically condemned unless the owner/landlord was prepared to spend money to bring it up to accepted 20th century standards. As yet, Kirklea had neither electricity nor sanitation, but it *did* have a cold water tap. Nennie's cottage didn't even have that.

The owner of these two-and-a-bit little houses lived in Herefordshire and though, more than once, he claimed to be about to do something with them, he never did. Father's offer to buy them was rejected and so that end of Victoria Place was to stand empty, mouldering and inadequately secured for the next two or three years. And then it happened.

Maybe it had been one of the big boys looking for a bit of 'winching' space; maybe it had been a passing tramp looking for a night's shelter; whoever was responsible, word quickly got about – the middle door was open. And so it was that Nennie's little cottage became part of our territory and though it had been cleared of her bits and pieces, there was a lot of debris around – old newspapers, periodicals, scraps of wood and so on.

We weren't vandals – not many children were in those days; if any charge could be laid against us, I suppose it would be that we were thoughtless of the consequences of quite a few of our actions. It wasn't long before the occasional fire was lit in the grate using material to hand – short, sharp bursts of flame that were over before any suspicious adult might feel inclined to investigate. Wiser heads would have wondered about the increasing amount of rubble and dust that had to be cleared from the grate before each cheerful blaze. The chimney was disintegrating and, at some point, an ember or two must have found their way in among the thatch where they snuggled down and smouldered contentedly.

Some of us were playing up the hill when we heard the clanging bell. We watched a fire-engine turn into the village and then saw the curls of smoke drifting up from the roof of the cottages. A mad, downhill dash began.

This was no straightforward fire. Its seat had been identified quickly enough (up by the chimney-head) but the firemen couldn't get at it because of the corrugated-iron. For the moment, it was a slow burner, but tearing off some of the sheets, as they'd have to, would turn it into a rager; tactics and timing became critical.

It was all going rather well and the blaze was close to being under control when ill luck took a hand. The hose's powerful jet which had been ripping into the flames, adding clouds of steam to the smoke and tossing lumps of burnt and unburnt thatch into the air, suddenly faltered, spluttered and fell to the ground in a diminishing and gentle arc. They'd run out of water.

Blairlogie was twenty-and-more years short of having a hydrant so the appliance had its own supply of water to start the fight. Knowing there was a burn in the village, it was assumed they'd be able to tap into it to re-stock the tanks to

Nennie Binnie (left) and her parents c. 1900.

Mr and Mrs Binnie outside their cottage at the end of Victoria Place, c.1900.

finish the job. Not so. At that time of year the burn was as dry as the blazing thatch – the cottages were doomed. While the tender trundled off to fill up at the River Forth – a three-mile round-trip away – those left behind attempted containment. It didn't work.

Much later, father was able to buy the land on which the cottages had stood. He extended Kirklea by building a double-garage (with sitting-room above) where the yard had been and the rest became part of an enlarged garden. Today, all that remains of that end of Victoria Place is a bit of rear wall – which now forms a terrace – and one other thing.

Above one of Kirklea's garage doors is a stone bearing the inscription AW – MC 1758. A marriage lintel, father had it built into the wall both as a memento and a wee joke – the garage was, after all, built in 1952. It came from the front door of the cottage originally owned by one, Alexander Williamson (tailor in Blairlogie) and his wife Margaret Clowe. The same cottage that Nennie Binnie was to occupy many years later.

2) Berryholes

Bicycles of the 1940s were singularly upright machines – racers apart – but Kate Gilmour's bike, already venerable, was rather more upright than most. Its exaggeratedly swept back handle-bars supported a wicker basket for her messages; the uppermost of the two diagonal front bars – structurally essential on ladies' bicycles – was deeply curved to allow for dignified movement when mounting and dismounting; the rear mudguard sported a double fan of strings down to the wheel's hub to stop long skirts (still worn then by countrywomen of a certain age) becoming entangled with spokes. It was, in short, a bike built for sedate, ladylike progress. With its owner sitting low in the broad saddle and pedalling with great caution, it was never in danger of achieving anything else.

At the entrance to the field immediately east of Witches' Craig caravan park is an area of uneven, stony ground and a solitary tree. This was the site of Berryholes – a steading

Berryholes, c.1950.
The gable window was that of my bedroom whenever I stayed the night.

occupied and worked by Kate, her younger sister Joan and an older brother, Willie (a widower returned to live with his sisters). I can't remember much about him and I don't think he played a big part in the running of the place; the two women seemed to do everything. Kate had charge of the house and things indoors, while Joan, a sturdy soul with the measured gait of one accustomed to the land, looked after the cow, the pig, the hens, the garden and anything else outdoors. As a source of extra income, Kate undertook domestic work for some in the village and, as often as mother was required in the Glasgow studios, Kate and her bike would make the short but slow journey from Berryholes to Kirklea where she did a bit of housework, kept me in good order and fed me mince on toast.

For much of its life, Berryholes performed a dual function – steading and public house. Lying a couple of hundred yards south of the old road and reached by a dead straight, narrow lane (the line of which is quite visible from higher ground behind the field when the light's right), it had been somewhat detached from its passing trade. When the new turnpike sliced through the ground immediately in front of it, Berryholes became a true roadside inn with a wee gusset of garden opposite – cast adrift by this arterial intrusion.

The O.S. map of 1864 shows the steading with the letters P.H. beside it, but by the time of the 1898 survey, the abbreviation's gone. At some time between these dates, Berryholes ceased to be an inn. I don't know exactly *when* this happened (mid-1870s I think), but I do know *why* it happened.

Lord George Ralph Abercromby, fourth and last of the dynastic line to rule most of that which could be seen from the family seat of Airthrey Castle, owned Berryholes and, therefore, any problems attached to its public house activities. Many landowners wouldn't countenance pubs on their estates; with a small army of gardeners, farm-workers, foresters and the like, the last thing they wanted was the temptation of a conveniently sited inn. Despite the Forbes-Mackenzie Act of 1853 which led to public houses closing at 11pm weekdays and all day Sunday, it was still possible for a man to bend the elbow for thirteen hours a day – probably longer in a rural inn such as Berryholes with its rudimentary overnight accommodation and opportunities for 'lockie-ins'. It would be no surprise were the interests of tenant and Abercromby to clash from time to time. They certainly did on one notable occasion – the one that finally led to its closure as a public house.

When a young forester failed to return to his lodgings one night or show up for work next day, eyebrows were raised and observations made, but little more than that. As two more nights and a day in between passed with neither sight nor sound of him, anxiety and concern increased sharply. When he still hadn't appeared by the third day, full-scale alarm set in. Search parties were organised to scour the furthest corners of the estate and, most difficult and time consuming of all, Airthrey's little loch was dragged. At the height of all this activity, its cause suddenly turned up – seedy, scruffy and severely hungover.

Clearly not a drinker of note (or Berryholes would have been investigated earlier) he had, nevertheless, fallen in with some bad company and become involved in a debauch of monumental proportions. This had left him comatose and undetected, lying behind a settle in the pub's side room – a state of suspended animation in which he seems to have existed for at least two days.

Abercromby and his factor were not at all pleased. I don't know if the young forester was given another chance; the tenant of Berryholes certainly wasn't. He and his were kicked out, the licence revoked and the tenancy of the place, as a steading only, offered to any interested party. In 1878, Kate's father, William Gilmour, became tenant farmer of Berryholes and the family connection endured until her death, at the age of 87, in 1970.

Tragically, the place was razed to the ground two years later.

3) The Orchard

Scree-running was great; tough on boots and tougher still on the runner should he lose his balance, but it made for an exhilaratingly rapid descent of a slope. Mind you, you had to pick your scree carefully. The best was the small, well-weathered stuff that moved easily. Bigger stones were no good;

they didn't glide and you were quite likely to do yourself a mischief trying to move them. If the scree was right, it was just like running down an escalator.

About half-way up the face of Castle Law is a precipice of quite impressive proportions (it certainly was from a child's perspective). According to my geologist neighbour, the rock is andesitic – a mixture of lavas and ashes. Possibly due to a fault near the top, much of the cliff face has weathered excessively and it's very unstable. The huge apron of scree at its foot was testimony to this water and frost induced deterioration. This was our favoured scree-running spot, but, nowadays, gorse, grass and bracken are steadily colonizing the area because of a loss of scree cover. Did we move that much?

Roughly seven hundred feet directly below the precipice is a large field of nearly three acres. Today, it's a little car-park with a big wilderness on either side but, years ago, the land was worked and lived on. A row of three 18th century cottages looked onto an open area of grazing-cum-growing ground and behind, between them and the boundary wall of the old road, was a substantial belt of fruit trees; because of these, the place was called The Orchard.

Obviously, the builders of the cottages didn't regard the cliff, looming far above, as a threat – actual or potential. They probably felt the undergrowth on Castle Law's lower slopes, along with the old road wall and the fruit trees beyond, would absorb and check the odd rolling stone. For long enough, this seems to have been the case but, ultimately, nature was to show them otherwise.

By 1935, only the easternmost of the cottages was occupied – by a widow, Mrs Mary McMillan, and her adult daughter, Catherine. (The latter was organist at Blairlogie Kirk.) Those to the west, having become empty and being quite devoid of any sort of amenity, were immediately condemned and their re-occupancy forbidden. They were already showing signs of neglect and dereliction.

August, 1935 had been wretchedly wet to the huge disgust of farmer and holidaymaker alike; Saturday, 24th was no different but Mrs McMillan and Catherine stayed dry and snug in the little cottage quite unaware that their very lives could soon be in danger. High up on the precipice, water streamed in and out of the myriad cracks and crevices as it had done for days; there was a sudden movement – a slight slippage of rock accompanied by a trickle of dross-like material. And then another...

Despite the rain, the dog still had to be walked and so it was that, on this dreich Saturday afternoon, Mr McLeish (Davie's father) entered The Orchard and started down the path leading to the hill.

The precipice, straight ahead and up, is a dominant feature – one that naturally attracts the eye – and Mr McLeish found himself studying it as he had done many times before. But this time was to be different. Horrified, he watched an immense boulder break away from the rockface and begin a ponderous tumbling, slithering downhill progress. By the time it reached the escarpment at the foot of the scree, it was clearly heading for the cottage and its unwitting occupants but, after careering briefly into thin air, it struck and flattened an immature ash tree. This fortunate impact succeeded in diverting the thing and, after demolishing a length of boundary wall and a couple of fruit trees, it came to rest six yards east of the cottage.

Mr McLeish's rush to inspect the monster (subsequently estimated to be a five-tonner) and tell the McMillans of their lucky escape turned into a very rapid retreat at a crashing, clatter from the scree slopes high above. A veritable bombardment of smaller stuff was bounding crazily downhill. These lesser rocks, lacking the sheer bulk of the boulder now lying at peace in the field, leapt and fizzed like things possessed. Being so many and having within several the capacity to damage and maim, they presented a sight almost as fearsome as the first. The boundary wall was breached at several points, and the back gate leading onto the hill disintegrated under the assault – but, miraculously, the cottage and its occupants remained unscathed.

I'm quite sure a potentially lethal near miss such as that would have had me away from there in very quick time. Amazingly, Mrs McMillan and Catherine didn't budge – but then, maybe it's *not* all that amazing. Where could they budge to? In order to buy a house elsewhere, they'd have to sell up, and while the land would be an attractive proposition, the primitive accommodation certainly wouldn't. Besides, immediately the McMillans moved out, the cottage would be condemned thus precluding anyone else from moving in – unless they were prepared to spend a *lot* of money on the place. In short, they were trapped. For five further years they had no option but to stay where they were but, mercifully, they were subjected to no more rock attacks; and then, by some means or other, they managed to get a house in Menstrie. Mrs McMillan still owned The Orchard as a property, but the row of cottages was now completely abandoned.

I think the mother must have died round about 1941 because the Valuation Roll for '42-'43 shows the land and empty houses at The Orchard as belonging to Catherine McMillan (spinster) of Ochil Road, Menstrie.

And then, along came Mr Evans.

Perhaps his job as senior storeman with Kork-N-Seal (a firm which made rather nifty bottle-tops for the drinks trade) was less than wholly satisfying; perhaps his life lacked the degree of independence many seek; perhaps it had always been his ambition to own and work a smallholding. Whichever, Mr Evans looked at The Orchard, saw potential, bought it and was immediately assailed by problem number one – accommodation for Mrs Evans and their children, Dougie, Mossie and baby Sheila. To do anything with the increasingly derelict cottages would prove prohibitively expensive; so much so that I doubt whether he even considered it. He elected, instead, to build his own house.

Wartime restrictions presented virtually everybody with shortages and difficulties of one kind or another – not least somebody wanting to build a new house – but Mr Evans was a resourceful man. He bought a small, half-timbered bungalow in Condorrat (near Cumbernauld), carefully dismantled and transported its component parts to Blairlogie and then, with the help of an accommodating brickie, put it all together again – right beside the huge boulder that had caused such concern eight years earlier. Wanting to spend every available minute

Bruce Stephens, Dougie, George Stephens and Mossie in front of exactly half of the Evans' bungalow. At the back of the symmetrical front (if you see what I mean) was a kitchen and bathroom.

The Orchard cottages.
The one on the right housed Mrs McMillan and Catherine. Mr Evans' bungalow was in the area of the first ten or so fence stobs to the right of the cottages.
The big house in the background is Blairlogie Park.

on his project, mr Evans camped in the McMillan's old cottage more or less for the duration of the reconstruction.

One of my Ensign Ful-Vue out-of-focus specials. It shows (roughly) a bit more of Mr Evans' bungalow.

The Orchard, being a bit less than three acres, was never going to be area enough to provide full independence for the Evans family; and bear in mind that a good chunk of the field was destined to become Blairlogie Thistle's football pitch. Pigs, poultry and a big vegetable patch meant they wouldn't go short of food, but Mr Evans was never in a position to give up the day job.

The bonds of boyhood – those pledges of unswerving loyalty and undying friendship – loosen and unravel as the years accumulate and circumstances change. So it was with us. By the mid-fifties, Blairlogie Thistle – Saturday nights at the pictures in Stirling with a threepenny poke of chips to round off the evening in style – the gang – adventures on the hills – raucous games in and around Blairmains or the village, were well behind us; some receding faster than others. New urges and priorities overtook us; new responsibilities loomed large in our respective lives; new friendships were formed in the wider world of work, apprenticeship, higher education or National Service. And so we drifted apart; not in a deliberate and unfriendly way, just gradually and casually. Of *course* we greeted each other happily whenever we met, but these meetings became more and more infrequent. Sad, but that's growing up for you.

The last time I saw the Evanses as a family was on the morning of Monday, July 14, 1958. I was at the bus stop, waiting for the 7.50 to Stirling and trying to make sense of the altered appearance of their bungalow roof, when the family car came into view heading for the main road – it swung in my direction. As the Lanchester slowly approached, I was surprised to see it held all five of them. They looked dreadful and my automatic wave became an uncertain, hesitant thing in the face of such obvious distress. There was a half-hearted response from Mossie, the driver. Mr Evans slumped beside him, left hand supporting his head in an attitude of utter despair and Dougie, Mrs Evans and Sheila sat in the back. Mother and daughter were weeping. That evening, I discovered why.

A lot of rain had fallen in the previous week, but the blanket of mist and cloud that settled on Castle Law throughout the weekend produced even more – *much* more. So, at the end of a particularly soggy Sunday, the Evanses retired for the night in preparation for the start of a new working week. Their world was, almost literally, about to collapse round their ears.

The crash and crack of rock on rock, louder by the second, was the only warning. Even had it been heard, it was far too late to do anything. Sleep became a confused and terrified wakefulness as a massive blow struck the felt and sarking roof causing it to sag above Sheila's shocked head. Shuddering thuds and shattering glass heralded the partial collapse of the rear wall and the total demolition of the bathroom. Short of being caught in a night air raid, I can think of nothing more terrifying than being on the receiving end of a night rock-fall. And, of course, they weren't to know if there was more to come. By the faint light in the northern sky, the rest of the night was spent emptying the broken house of its contents and then huddling together in the car until such time as relatives they could stay with would be up and about. It's little wonder Mr Evans looked a defeated man as he and his family passed me on that Monday morning. The wee bungalow he'd raised with such high hopes, fifteen years earlier, was now being abandoned to the vagaries of nature.

Today, there's not a single trace of the little house or the old cottages nearby; it's as if they had never existed.

Bobby's Ball

Bobby was a bit older than the rest of us and the hormonal activity that was beginning to surprise and delight our younger bodies had, virtually, completed its task in his. Bobby was into girls – if you see what I mean. Not for him the noisy games of 'kick-the-can' or 'raleaso' or the promising, but invariably disappointing, 'truths-and-dares' that we were wont to play with the girls of the village. He was looking for a different kind of game. Nothing beastly, of course; no more than a nudging, winking perambulation of flirtatious youth wandering the douce streets of Stirling – his preferred winching ground since it was out of range of the prying eyes and tell-tale tongue of his younger sister, Nan.

On a particularly pleasant Saturday evening of a late spring, when our thoughts, naturally, turned to the possible delights of a kick-about, Bobby's preference for the pursuit of a girl rather than a ball presented us with a problem. Having suffered grievous harm under the chassis of a co-op van, my football was at the cobbler's and somebody else's was in an equally sad state. This only left Bobby's ball. A consultation at his front door proved less than successful.

"Fancy a gemm, Bobby?"

"Naw!"

"How no' ?"

"Ah'm winchin' the night."

"Can we get a len o' yer ba' ?"

"Naw!"

"How no' ?"

"Yiz'll mebbies bust it."

Protestations to the effect that, under our astute stewardship, this couldn't possibly happen fell on singularly unimpressed ears. So, with nothing better to do, we accompanied Bobby to that point accepted by all parties as the bus stop for Stirling although, at that time, there was no official sign to indicate this. Desultory chat followed.

In those days, Saturday night was the main event of the week and, with a variety of entertainments provided by its four cinemas, dance hall and many pubs, a lot of people headed for Stirling.

Being the last link in the chain of Hillfoots' settlements, Blairlogie wasn't the best place to catch a Saturday evening bus – despite the fact that there were more of them about then than now. From first sighting to stopping place, the would-be passenger had a hundred yards or so in which to assess the likelihood of being picked up. If the window to the right of the driver's cab was black, that meant people were standing – even on the platform. No chance! If, on the other hand, daylight could be seen through the same window, people either weren't standing or, at least, there were fewer of them. Every chance! To Bobby's obvious gloom and our concealed glee, two black-windowed buses had already thundered by. This double blow to his winching hopes, and his response to it, revived our footballing ones...

"If the next yin disnae stop, ah'll away an' change an' we'll hae a gemm."

And here it was now. To our dismay, we could see daylight through the all important window; a quick look passed between us; an unspoken idea seemed to be forming.

When you're a going-on-sixteen-year-old, you don't make your wishes known to the driver by sticking out your hand – that's for bairns an' auld wifies. A roll of the shoulders, a hitch of the breeks and a step forward is the manly way. This last movement, of course, conveniently removed us from Bobby's line of vision and his attention. Desperate times call for desperate measures. We stood at his back like a chorus-line and we reacted like one. Each raised a right hand and with a sweeping movement, waved the bus on. It maintained its speed. Too late, manliness was forgotten and a hand shot out. The double-decker roared past. Bobby's jaw slackened then tightened sufficiently to form and expel one of those words – the kind grown-ups didn't like you to use.

"Did y'see that?"

"Aye, Bobby. Thon's terrible!"

Two kicked stones, a different bad word and a resigned shrug of the shoulders later, he turned for home.

"Right; see yiz at the park in ten minutes."

We moved in that direction – fine pleased with ourselves.

Past Villagers

Concerning some of those adults who populated our childhood and left an impression of one sort or another.

My first pal was about sixty years older than me and our friendship formed as a result of a brick falling on my big toe – an action generating a degree of pain and a great deal of noise.

It was 1941 and we'd not long moved into Kirklea Cottage which, in order to meet the habitation standards demanded by Stirling County Council, was undergoing great works. This involved chaos inside and fascinating piles of sand and bricks outside. Having decided to move one of the latter from A to B, it fell from my less than firm grasp straight on to my off side big toe. This, in common with the other toes, was exposed to the world at large – and bricks in particular – due to a wartime economy. To get more wear out of things like sandals when they were having difficulty containing growing feet, the toe-caps were cut off – a simple and effective remedy, but one affording no protection against falling bricks.

As the red mist cleared and the bellowing diminished, I was surprised to discover that the words and sounds of comfort were being administered, not by my mother – she was a bit late on the scene – but by the old lady I'd acknowledged several times before when she'd been walking her dogs. She, the dogs and I became friends.

Mrs Morris, Tomaca to her intimates though I haven't

the faintest idea why, was one of several kenspeckle figures to inhabit Blairlogie in the 1940s. Her late father had been a landowner of some consequence on Mull, so her background was gentrified but without a trace of the condescension that can sometimes accompany such status. She was just a thoroughly nice person. Divorced, she lived in Montana Cottage, in the square, as a sub-tenant of her friend Mrs 'Charlie' Jauncey who shared accommodation in Montague Cottage (now Blairlogie House Hotel) with Mme Guinevere De Beaumont. This lady was, allegedly, the estranged wife of the pretender to the throne of France. Now, that's kenspeckle!

Tomaca's dogs were Bronx, an English bull-terrier of occasionally mean spirit – as more than one village cat found to its cost – and Gorm (Gaelic = blue), an eccentric Dalmatian named after his blue eye; the other was brown. I think Gorm was deaf – a condition supposedly afflicting twenty per cent of his breed. Certainly he was a nervous dog and reacted badly to surprise, which leads nicely to another weel kent figure of the time. A very short one.

* * *

Wee K. could only be described as a dwarf. Head and trunk were pretty normal, but the limbs were less so – especially the short and very bowed legs. He was a miner and, therefore, perfectly designed for his job; I imagine there was hardly a coal-face that he couldn't work while standing. He cycled to and from Manor Powis pit on a bike best described as small adult's or large child's and Wee K. in cycling mode was one of life's more spectacular sights. So Gorm thought.

Until Tomaca timed the walks to avoid such confrontations, there were two or three occasions when we, walking down Manor Loan, suddenly met Wee K. cycling up. This apparition, lurching wildly from side to side on the saddle, was too much for Gorm. Ears flat, tail between legs, he raced round and round the, by now, wobbling figure in a yelping frenzy to Tomaca's consternation and Wee K.'s severe displeasure – expressed loudly and colourfully. For several reasons, not least his attitude to my friend Gorm, he was one I preferred to avoid where possible.

* * *

Mr and Mrs William Kennedy, owners and postmaster/mistress of Blairlogie's shop-cum-post office, were also small. Not as small as Wee K., but small – especially Mrs Kennedy. As a child, and a bit short on stature myself, I would often take my mother's list of messages down to the little shop and hand it over to its proprietrix. Our eyes were just able to meet from our respective sides of the counter but, from time to time, some of the rest of Mrs Kennedy would come into view, before disappearing again, as she clambered on and off various boxes or steps to reach items more than five feet above floor-level.

When Peggy Dawson ran the village's first post office, mail was delivered by a man who walked from Stirling with three bags; one each for Blairlogie, Menstrie and Alva. There, he rested his feet 'til the afternoon before making the return journey, collecting the bags with mail for Stirling on the way. Daily? I don't know, but a few times a week I should imagine. He must have been one fit postman.

When William Kennedy ran the village's second post office, things had moved on a bit. Now, the morning mail was dropped off by one of Alexander's buses and, in the afternoon, Mr Kennedy would hand a bag to the conductress of a prescribed bus bound for Stirling. That was the easy bit. His other duties were much more onerous because, as well as being post*master*, he was also post*man* – and his was a broad patch. Donning the uniform and mounting the red bike with its front shelf for mail bags, he delivered post to the village and outlying parts in and around the loans of Powis, Manor and Gogar – emptying the various boxes on the way. Again, that was the easy bit, because his area also included parts of Sherrifmuir's uplands; possibly Cauldhame and surrounds but, certainly, Jerah on the old road behind Dumyat. Bizarrely, the latter had a small post-box at the summit which Mr Kennedy emptied twice a week in pre-war summers, franking each postcard with a special

'Dumyat' stamp. No, he didn't cycle up.

As if he hadn't spent enough time in the saddle, during the bowling season he would ride along to Menstrie for a game on most evenings. For this, he used his civvy bike – a douce, black affair.

* * *

In summer, when the evenings seemed to go on forever, Jimmy Houston would sit on his front door step, clay pipe in mouth, curls of smoke about his head. Contented. Despite the bulk of Blair House to the front, he actually had quite a good, distant view because his door step was higher up than most.

Reached by an external staircase, Jimmy and his sister Catherine lived in the upper floor of Crowsteps – in two tiny rooms without an amenity between them and not much more in the way of furniture. For instance, there was only one bed and, since they were brother and sister with all the implications of that relationship, Jimmy had it – no doubt at Catherine's insistence. It may seem unfair, but that's the way it was in those days; the man came first in all things. For years, Catherine slept in a chair by the fireside until an appalled newcomer – Mrs Bampton – discovered how things were. A small single bed was quickly provided for the sister, so at least her subsequent sleep could be of the horizontal variety.

Jimmy's stocky, bunneted figure, setting out on his twice daily walk, was part of the village scene and those he met were greeted with a careful nod and a slow, shy smile on his heavily stubbled face. But it wasn't always so.

In common with many of his generation, Jimmy had fought on the grim and bloody fields of the First World War and though he was fortunate enough to remain physically intact, he'd been left with a mental scar that stayed with him 'til he died. Jimmy was shell-shocked. A sudden and loud noise could bring memories and images flooding into his confused mind and, if he happened to be out walking, the transformation was frightening – especially to us children. The mild, shy man instantly became a roaring, cursing cratur, arms beating violently at things only he could see. But then, quite quickly, the ghosts would go, the terror would subside and, shy smile restored, the walk would continue as if nothing had happened.

* * *

Over thirty years ago, my father bought the single-storey cottage abutting upon the lean-to containing our kitchen and bathroom. It now forms part of Kirklea but for many years, and under its own name of Burnside Cottage, it was the home of Willie and Minnie Henderson – a cheery and neighbourly couple.

Willie was a busy man – one you didn't see all that often. A joiner and undertaker to trade, he seemed to spend all day at his workshop in the old Meal Mill up at the back of Menstrie. And then there were his other commitments – the Menstrie Scouts and Blairlogie Kirk; with the latter he was beadle and general factotum. You really only ever saw him doing a bit of gardening at the weekend or, perhaps, of a pleasant summer evening, sitting with Minnie on the bench in front of their garden wall; he smoking his pipe, she knitting and both of them watching the Blairlogie bit of the world going by. Occasionally, he might be heard if not seen. Willie had a fine tenor voice, one that was put to good use in the Kirk choir, and he could sometimes be overheard practising in the end room of their little cottage – the 'best' room – accompanying himself on an old and very asthmatic harmonium. I didn't, therefore, have much to do with Willie which was probably to his advantage, but Minnie I got to know well; initially through a coat and some gooseberries.

Clothing coupons, and their management, were a constant headache for the wartime housewife and mother. When buying clothes for children, the golden rule was allow-for-growth – a principle my mother understood well but one she was inclined to overdo; notably so on one occasion.

I needed a coat so, sufficient coupons having been collected and counted, I was taken to get it. Even the enthusiastic saleswoman was looking doubtful by the time the purchase had been made. My slight figure was draped in a garment which, if re-designed, could have made me a modest tent. Sleeves folded in on themselves solved one problem but nothing, immediately, could be done about the coat-skirt; this brushed my ankles – well, almost. It didn't bother me though, because I had not yet encountered that most damaging digit – a child's pointing finger of ridicule. By golly, once that's experienced, you soon learn to consider how you look in the eyes of your peers. Anyway, returning home from Stirling, my small hand in my mother's larger one, my big coat moving quite independently of me, we passed Minnie chatting to a neighbour. Both were elderly and both slightly deaf, so Minnie's aside came across rather more clearly than she had, presumably, intended...

"Puir bairn. Fancy daein' that tae 'im." They probably didn't hear my mother's snort.

Going out to play some little while later, I saw Minnie in her garden and she saw me...

"Here, sonny. Hae some o' these." From her apron pocket she produced a handful of gooseberries – golden, hairless, soft, delicious. Clearly, a reward for putting up with that coat.

After Willie died, father took it upon himself to keep an eye on Minnie who was, by now, in her late seventies – to be a good neighbour, in fact. On informing him that she was vexed by a water-stain on her 'best' room ceiling, he immediately volunteered to investigate.

Minnie's cottage is narrow but long, and there's a surprising amount of roof-space. Needless to say, the source of the problem appeared to be at the far end. A small glow from the open trapdoor apart, it was pitch dark, musty and not a little eery in a mid-18th century kind of way. Father, on hands and knees, moved from joist to joist with great care – illumination provided by a guttering candle which he dragged along with him. More than half-way through his painful journey, a sudden sound from behind nearly sent a hand and knee crashing through the ceiling. Turning, in some horror, to ward off the phantom or giant rat or whatever, he was astonished to see the small figure of Minnie nimbly moving across the joists,

Minnie Henderson (oldest inhabitant in 1953) receiving a bouquet and a splendid curtsy from Helen Irvine (one of the younger ones) on the occasion of the planting of the Coronation cherry tree. Behind is Mr James Loudon.

hands swinging from the cross-ties above her head...

"Jist wanted tae see y'were a' richt, Mr Kelsall."

Collapse of paternal party.

Footnote: There's an indirect memorial to Minnie Henderson in the shape of her garden (now the village garden) and, next to it, the cherry-blossom tree which commemorates the Queen's coronation. As Blairlogie's oldest inhabitant at the time, Minnie took the lead in the planting ceremony.

In Conclusion

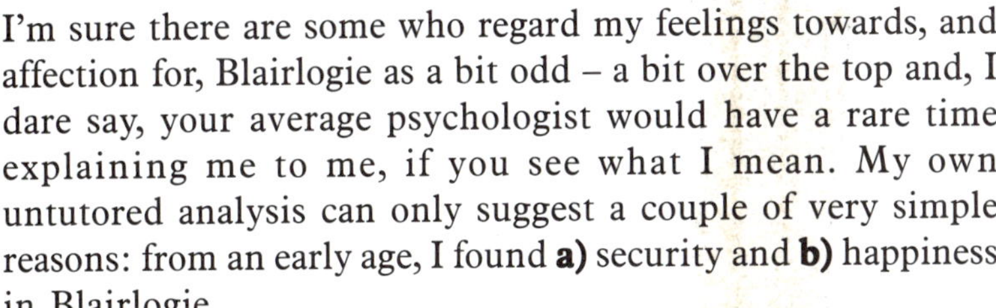

I'm sure there are some who regard my feelings towards, and affection for, Blairlogie as a bit odd – a bit over the top and, I dare say, your average psychologist would have a rare time explaining me to me, if you see what I mean. My own untutored analysis can only suggest a couple of very simple reasons: from an early age, I found **a)** security and **b)** happiness in Blairlogie.

I suppose infants can be unsettled by a moderately itinerant existence such as ours was and, certainly, separation from one's parents is not a terribly good idea – even one as temporary as my retreat to Mary's parental farm to escape Hitler's intentions. And so I was five before our little family started to put down roots when we moved to Blairlogie; even then, there was another separation to come.

With the exception of her one cold tap, Kirklea was two hundred years behind the times and the drastic surgery required to bring her, creaking and groaning, into the mid-20th century was deemed unsafe and unhealthy for me. I became, for a short while, a weekly boarder at a small school near Balfron – a wretched period in my young life and one that quickly taught me to associate the western end of the Ochils with home. As the Friday afternoon bus approached it, my heart soared; as it receded on Sunday's return, my heart sank like a wee stone. In truth, this episode lasted no more than two or three months, but it had a salutary effect on us all. Clearly, my subsequent education would never involve boarding-schools. With security now established, happiness had every chance of flourishing.

An only child, and one totally unversed in even the most primitive social skills, I was shyly wary of those of my own age who lived nearby but, gradually, contact was made – communications were established – friendships formed. Being such a small group in such a small community, we were lucky that there wasn't a single 'baddie' in our number to cause distress or problems; we all got on splendidly – the odd tiff or scrap apart. This good fortune guaranteed the happiness that pervaded our Blairlogie boyhood.

To grow up in the place was a privilege. To grow old in it is another.